ROCKMONT COLLEGE

BUSINESS PLAN FOR AMERICA

BUSINESS PLAN FOR AMERICA

AN ENTREPRENEUR'S MANIFESTO

Don Gevirtz

A Boston Book/G. P. Putnam's Sons
New York

Copyright © 1984 by Don Gevirtz
All rights reserved. This book, or parts thereof, may not be reproduced in
any form without permission in writing from the publisher. Published on
the same day in Canada by General Publishing Co. Limited, Toronto.

Library of Congress Cataloging in Publication Data

Gevirtz, Don.
    Business plan for America.

    "A Boston book."
    1. Small business—United States—Management.
    2. Entrepreneur. I. Title.
    HD62.7.G48   1984   658.4'2   83-2114
    ISBN 0-399-12844-1

PRINTED IN THE UNITED STATES OF AMERICA

ACKNOWLEDGMENTS

In the early years of my business career, I was not pleased to be called an entrepreneur. That label did not achieve respectability until our economy got in trouble in the 1970s. As an entrepreneur, I have had at least two major successes and at least two failures. The failures hurt much more than the successes felt good.

As the economy began to stumble ten years ago, it became clear to me that the entrepreneur was its salvation, and that there were serious political consequences to entrepreneurs coming together to seek political power. I hope this book encourages that political unification.

Since I am an entrepreneur and not an author by profession, this book could not have been created without a major collaborator. Although he has withdrawn from the project and requested anonymity, I must acknowledge his invaluable contribution in writing *Business Plan for America.*

From the beginning it was a humbling experience for both of us. Although we had firsthand experience in entrepreneurship, one in industry and finance and the other as an author and journalist, it would have been impossible to connect these experiences with the complex issues in this book without the assistance of many friends and colleagues.

The major inspiration and most important advisor, particularly with regard to entrepreneurial economic policies and their political linkage, was Dr. John M. Albertine, President of the American Business Conference. Another close friend who was instrumental in shaping the scenario for communicating the ideas in this book was Paul Spindler. Central to the creative process was the excellent research work performed by Mark Benham, and the staff of the Community Information Project in Los Angeles, in particular Martin Burns and Dan Leighton. In reference to Japan and East Asian issues, I was fortunate to have the assistance and advice of Yoriko Kishimoto of Japan Pacific Associates, Palo Alto, California. Finally, I pay special honor to the essential work of David Pardo, Ph.D. candidate in the Department of Finance, University of Southern California, whose work in the area of finance and European issues was both valuable and stimulating.

Beyond my own research team, I was given considerable aid by various experts who, in their own special fields of interest, gave cheerfully of themselves and their time. In the area of politics, special mention should be made of Walter Stults of the National Association of Small Business Investment Companies; Mike McKevitt and Denny Dennis of the National Federation of Independent Business; Dr. Otis Graham of the University of North Carolina; Al From of the House Democratic Caucus; Louis Krauthoff of the Joint Economic Committee; Congressman Edward Zschau of California; Kent Hughes of U.S. Senator Gary Hart's staff; Herb Liebenson of the National Small Business Association; Bruce Freed of the House Small Business Committee staff; Alan Neece of Neece-Cator Associates; Ken Haggerty of the American Electronics Association; Congressman Gillis Long; and Robert Poole of the Reason Foundation.

In the area of high technology and regional development, I owe much to Regis McKenna of Regis McKenna Public Relations in Palo Alto; Hank Riggs of the Stanford University School of Engineering and Engineering Management; Stan Golder of Golder, Thoma; Dimitri d'Arbeloff of Millipore Corporation; Craig Burr, Bill Egan, and Jean Deleage of Burr, Egan, and Deleage; Jim Howell, Chief Economist, First National Bank of Boston; and Brian Haslett of Venture Economics. The section on the Midwest was greatly enhanced by the sage advice of Frank Cassell of Northwestern University; Elizabeth Hollander of the Metropolitan Housing and Planning Council of Chicago; David P. Kanicke, editor, *Modern Casting*; Leo McDonough, Executive Vice-President, Smaller

Manufacturers' Council of Pittsburgh; Tom Hazen of the Illinois State Department of Commerce and Community Affairs; Joseph C. Wyman of Shearson-American Express; Father Thomas Hogan of Fordham University; Alex Carroll, Thompson McKinnon Securities, Indianapolis; Joseph Briganti, Senior Vice-President, Foothill Capital Corporation, Chicago; David Baker of the Illinois State Chamber of Commerce; Joel Hirshhorn of the Office of Technology Assessment; Ron Grzywinski of South Shore Bank; Joan Ross Walsky of the National Association of Manufacturers; Professor Douglas Lamont of Roosevelt University; Jack Bell of the National Machining and Tooling Association; and Steve Daly, Mayor of Kokomo, Indiana.

In the area of finance I was equally fortunate to have access to the wisdom of Tom Ruhm and Peter Bancroft of Bessemer Securities, New York; Robert Davidoff of Carl Marks; author Lawrence Litvack; James Vitarello from the office of Controller of the Currency, Washington, DC; Carl Schmitt of the University National Bank and Trust Company of Palo Alto; author Derek "Pete" Hanson; Stan Shuman of Allen and Company; bank consultant Tracy Herrick; Roger Altman of Lehman Brothers Kuhn Loeb; Marc Reinganum of the Graduate School of Finance, University of Southern California; Dick Gunther and Dr. Arthur Malin. Special thanks also to Gary Wehrle, Executive Vice-President of the Foothill Group, Los Angeles, for their timely and informative comments on the manuscript. For the section dealing with overseas issues I am greatly indebted to Takaski Sakai, Executive Vice-President, C. Itoh and Company, USA; Jean Paul Ange and the staff of the French Industrial Development Agency; Professor Jeffrey Hart of the University of Indiana; Aki Tsurukame of California Coordinators, Los Angeles; and Frank Kline of Pacific Technology Venture Management, San Francisco.

Finally, several people contributed to the presentation of broader issues throughout the book. Among the most notable is David Birch of MIT, whose work on job creation helped clear the path that I and hopefully others will follow; Modesto Maidique of Stanford University, whose careful reading of the manuscript proved absolutely invaluable, particularly concerning the process of industrial innovation and management; Michael Kieschnieck of the Working Assets Management Fund; Professor Warren Bennis of the University of Southern California; and veteran civil servant Robert Rosenberg of Sacramento who reminded me of the important role government could play even in the most entrepreneurial economy. I would also like to pay my respects to the "Berkeley Mafia"—the Berkeley Roundtable on the International Economy including John Zysman, Mike Borrus, Steve Cohen, and Laura Tyson—to whose vision for American public policy I owe a tremendous and lasting debt. And I single out my business partner, John Nickoll, President of the Foothill Group, who has shared with me and contributed mightily to fourteen years of the gut entrepreneurial experience.

In closing, I would like to acknowledge the hundreds of people whose contributions have not been cited here. I hope they know how deeply I appreciate their efforts. But I would be remiss if I did not extend my heartfelt thanks to those friends who, as professional colleagues, played a central role in keeping the project afloat at all stages including Sylvia Finkel, Jude Dumas, and Chris Sturman of the Foothill Group; my various editorial colleagues, Joel Garreau of *The Washington Post*, Brad Ketchum and George Gendron of *Inc.*; Charles Hartman of Boston Books; and Christine Schillig of G. P. Putnam's Sons who, most miraculously of all, actually brought this work to print. My heartfelt thanks to you all.

To my wife, Marilyn Gevirtz —
who somehow endured it all, lovingly, and who was the
litmus test of the manifesto.

CONTENTS

1

THE HUMAN FACTOR

At first glance, 1800 McCall Street looks like an advertisement for industrial obsolescence—a dull-red brick building amid the rusty railroad tracks and potholed streets of Dayton's decaying west side. Yet today, for the first time in three years, life is stirring inside the one-hundred-year-old foundry. Idle hands that for years listlessly switched television dials now mold and shape the gray iron bars into pipe castings.

Bill Guise took over the old foundry back in 1982, largely because no one else wanted it. On the wrong side of town, an artifact of the 19th-century Industrial Revolution, Kuhns Foundry seems to violate virtually every canon of economic fashion. Its owner, an Indiana-based conglomerate pressed by the recession, virtually begged Guise to take it off their hands. To them, ownership of the old foundry meant red ink running on into infinity. But to the 57-year-old metallurgist who had worked as a manager at the foundry thirty years earlier, Kuhns stood out as a challenge, a final chance to achieve his peculiar entrepreneurial dream:

I've had my sanity seriously questioned about this. Places like Kuhns become unfashionable and practically are given away to a bunch of crazies who can make money in the same damned marketplace. Your conglomerate analysts and accountants might never understand it but I'm convinced this is the wave of the future.

The new life at 1800 McCall Street illustrates just one small piece of a growing transformation of the American economy. Often building upon the discards of the giants—plants abandoned, markets ignored, ideas rejected—millions of American entrepreneurs are injecting new spirit into an economy that has grown increasingly listless over the past decade. Although sometimes linked to the development of new technology, as in the case of Apple Computers, America's entrepreneurial success stories owe as much to the commitment of the individual, the intangible "human factor" capable of turning a perennial money loser into a profitable venture. Amid the clutter of his beloved 19th-century machinery, Ken Guise explains:

> The entrepreneur is the missing link, the unpredictable element in the economic equation. Everyone in this plant has their future, their lives invested in this place. It has to work or we're out in the streets. We have to do what no one else is doing. And why? Because there's money, even in iron, by staying relatively small and being very smart.

Through being small and smart, Ken Guise and millions of other American entrepreneurs are rapidly disproving the old notions of economies of scale, scientific management, and the impregnability of big business long dominant in economic thinking. When Guise and his "band of crazies" took over Kuhns, for instance, their hard assets consisted of a creaky, cobwebbed plant, a Doberman pinscher, and some rusty old machinery. In less than a year, however, Guise found a market niche for iron pipe castings that no large company had bothered to pursue. Relentlessly chasing potential customers across the country, Guise achieved sales of over $1 million by the end of his first year in business. Thirty-five people, half of them from the predominantly black west side, suddenly found work in the drafty old mill. Within a few years, Guise expects annual sales to reach over $10 million and to employ over 400 workers. The spirit at Kuhns reflects a great transformation now sweeping the American economy. Armed with only a small amount of capital, with the weight of government regulation and taxation against them, America's entrepreneurs over the past decade have produced virtually all the nation's new private sector jobs and the bulk of its innovations while increasingly earning far higher returns on equity. In the process, they are moving American capitalism past the era of corporate leviathans and toward a new entrepreneurial configuration. Ken Guise, looking more the part of a janitor than an executive in his gray workman's pants, predicts confidently:

> If the sixties and the seventies were the era of mergers and acquisitions, I think the eighties will be an era of divestitures. The giants cannot hold. They cannot motivate like us because they are in a constant state of compromise. They are into so many things and have more concerns than the human mind can conceive. They have so many problems they can only see them in a pale shade of gray.
>
> Here people clearly see the challenge before them. There's no choice but to meet it. This may not be a glamour industry but that doesn't mean we can't make a hell of a run at it. The motivation is the individual challenge. No big organization yet has found a way to beat that.

THE TWILIGHT OF THE GIANTS

The American economy today stands at the end of an epoch. For nearly a century, the nation moved steadily in the direction of giantism—toward ever greater concentrations of economic and political power. But by the early 1960s, Americans began losing faith in mammoth business institutions. In the twenty-five years between 1955 and 1980 public approval for the institutions of big business dropped from 80 percent to less than 20 percent.[1] Disenchantment with giantism expressed itself in numerous ways, from the antiauthoritarian spirit of the 1960s campus rebellions to a resurgent conservative movement seeking to recapture the economic individualism that had characterized the nation's past.

But more than anything else, this mounting disaffection reflected deep-seated personal changes transcending the easy, often irrelevant categories of politics. The counterculture of the 1960s and 1970s, so often identified with the "left," did not usher in a new anticapitalist spirit. As Harvard Business School's George Cabot Lodge notes, the makers of the campus rebellions represented "a return to individualism in its purest and most extreme form." Like the pioneer capitalists of the 19th century, the sixties rebels increasingly resented the restraints inherent in hierarchical business organizations; between 1968 and 1976, the percentage of Americans who would willingly submit to being "bossed around" dropped from 56 to 36 percent.[2]

During the last fifteen years, this growing antiauthoritarian streak has expressed itself in distinctly capitalist forms. While at the onset of the 1960s new business formations stood at 180,000 per year, they increased steadily during the 1970s and reached over 600,000 a year by 1981, an unprecedented threefold increase. At the same time the number of self-employed persons, declining for most of the nation's history, also jumped dramatically from 5.1 million in 1970 to over 6.6 million ten years later.[3] Looking back at the influence of the 1960s, Berkeley graduate Jared Anderson who founded Valid Logic, a small high-technology firm across the Bay in Silicon Valley, put his boots up on his desk and explained:

> I went to school with [free speech movement leader] Mario Savio and had tear gas thrown at me. I went through all those lifestyle changes; it had a big psychological impact on me. I had wanted to be a physics professor but in the 1960s I learned that professors had no power. I figured I didn't want to be part of a bureaucracy.
>
> I could have worked for Phillips or something like it for the rest of my life but I like working in this start-up environment. There's a lot of juices flowing. I guess you can say I'm an excitement junkie.

Largely due to "excitement junkies" like Anderson, small and medium-sized companies are now emerging as the key creative force in the nation's economy. Between 1969 and 1976 small firms with less than twenty employees created as many as two-thirds of all the nation's new jobs, according to in-depth studies by MIT Professor David Birch. Another study, based on IRS statistics, states that small and medium-sized companies with under 500 employees produced as many as three-quarters of the new jobs.[4] In marked contrast, the Fortune 500 firms, after doubling their number of jobs between 1954 and 1970, failed to generate any new jobs and actually began reducing their domestic payrolls. As the 1980s began, this trend intensified with over 1.3 million workers laid off by giant firms that reduced their work forces to levels below those of ten years earlier.[5]

This represents a dramatic change in where Americans find their employment opportunities. Between 1965 and 1980 the number of Americans working in firms of over 500 employees dropped markedly, while those involved in smaller-scale businesses with fewer than 250 employees climbed to nearly 70 percent of the total work force. Even on the industrial front the trend has been toward smaller firms; factory size, averaging nearly 50 employees in 1947, dropped to under 44 in 1972. During the past ten years, as big business sharply curtailed manufacturing employees, small firms have consistently boosted their payrolls and reversed the long-standing trend toward the concentration of industrial assets.[6]

In their quest for economic independence, America's new entrepreneurs reflect the traditional character of American capitalism. No other country has been such a beacon to the world's dreamers and outsiders seeking the brass ring of business success. Where capitalism in most countries, notably Great Britain, France, and Germany, has become increasingly dominated by a fixed industrial aristocracy, in America the individual entrepreneur has continued to challenge the well-heeled, firmly entrenched economic hegemony.

To a large extent, this fiercely independent spirit grew out of the pioneers' struggle to develop the western frontier. In a vast land where the field for individual enterprise—the family farm, the small shop or factory—seemed limitless, the elitist traditions of Europe quickly dissipated. In its place a new, distinctive American capitalism arose. As the historian Frederick Jackson Turner observed:

> American democracy came from the forest; and its destiny drove it to material conquests; but the materialism of the pioneer was not the dull contented materialism of an old and fixed society. Both the native settler and the European immigrant saw in the free and competitive movement of the frontier the chance to break the bondage of social rank, and rise to a higher plane of existence.[7]

In their quest for this "higher plane of existence," the pioneers and other entrepreneurs throughout America's history have repeatedly struggled against those seeking to impose a European-style order. Despite the assertions of such modern-day Tories as George Gilder, the role of the rich and established forces has not been oriented predominantly toward "fostering opportunities for the classes below them."[8] In reality most new entrepreneurs have faced the determined opposition of the entrenched powers. Though the old elite at times has financed some of the new ventures, the great entrepreneurial parvenus—from Andrew Carnegie and Henry Ford to Howard Hughes—spent the most critical years of their early careers at war with established elites of their day. In fact the entrepreneurial struggle in the United States has been essentially a process of continuous revolution with each new wave of business overthrowing successful earlier ones.

The latest expression of this continuous revolution is the growing conflict between the large, established corporate interests and the new entrepreneurial forces. First emerging at the conclusion of the Civil War as a group of determined entrepreneurs—including Southern Pacific founder Leland Stanford, Andrew Carnegie, J. P. Morgan, and scores of others—today's established companies spearheaded the transformation of a pastoral America into an industrial powerhouse. Overcoming the resistance of local business elites, craft guilds, and agriculturalists, they created a new kind of society dominated by large industrial corporations, mass marketing, and mass production.

Under this new industrial order, the vision of the frontier capitalists—of a republic of small proprietors—seemed hopelessly archaic. As corporations burgeoned and then combined into even greater units, the percentage of self-employed Americans dropped from 80 percent in 1780 to a mere 9 percent in 1970. By 1970 the 200 largest firms held some 60 percent of all the nation's manufacturing assets.[9]

The emergence of these great corporations, along with the closing of the nation's western frontier, led many perceptive observers to conclude that individualism had little place in the future of American capitalism. As early as the 1940s economist Joseph Schumpeter observed that this giantism had already created a massive "decline in the entrepreneurial function" and would lead ultimately to the triumph of a "sober kind of socialism."[10]

Like his Harvard colleague Schumpeter, sociologist Pitirim Sorokin saw the rulers of giant capitalism as "the prime agents" of a new, emerging economic collectivism. However, in Sorokin's view the entrepreneur was not being replaced by socialist commissars, but by a new "managerial aristocracy" nurtured to tend the giant corporations emerging in the early years of this century.[11] Products of bureaucratic as opposed to entrepreneurial culture, these managers retained little of the individual drive and creativity of the old entrepreneurs. Shortly before his death in 1919, Andrew Carnegie stated bluntly:

> You have the dividing line between the businessman and the non-businessman; one is the master and depends on profits, the other a servant and depends on salary. . . . I do not believe that even the Presidents of these corporations, being only salaried men, are to be classified as businessmen at all.[12]

With the passing of Carnegie and entrepreneurial founders like him, these "salaried men" soon transformed such companies as U.S. Steel, General Electric, and General Motors into vast, self-perpetuating bureaucracies, collectivist mentalities in the service of capitalist objectives. To them, the old-fashioned entrepreneur, building his firm upon an individualist vision, was as antiquated as the western gunslinger. Frederick Taylor, the efficiency expert whose teaching had profound impact on corporate managers, prophesied: "In the future it will be appreciated that our leaders must be trained right, and that no great man can hope to compete with a number of ordinary men who have been properly organized."[13]

This conception of business organization, almost completely devoid of the individualist "human factor," reached its apotheosis in the late 1960s. With the rise of the conglomerate, the rationalization of business extended beyond product lines; companies were swallowed wholesale whether or not they had anything to do with the acquirer's original line of business. Between 1960 and 1968, the annual number of mergers jumped from 844 to over 2400, with a skyrocketing price tag from $1.7 billion to over $13 billion. By 1969, large corporate mergers, many of them by conglomerates, equaled more than *one third* of the total capital expenditures made by mining and manufacturing firms.[14]

Though offended by some of the more avaricious conglomerates, few leading intellectuals challenged the growing trend toward corporate giantism. Some, like Daniel Bell, saw in these increasingly complex, technologically sophisticated organizations the harbingers of a new "post-industrial economy" presiding over a "new dominant class" of scientists, engineers, technocrats, and, of course, university-based intellectuals. In an era of massive technological change, as epitomized by the space program, economists such as John Kenneth Galbraith argued that only huge corporations possessed the sophistication to apply science to industry. In this new economic order, Galbraith assigned virtually no role to the entrepreneur:

There is no more pleasant fiction than that technical change is the product of the matchless ingenuity of the small man forced to employ his wits to better his neighbor. Unhappily, it is a fic-

tion. Technical development has long since become the preserve of the scientist and the engineer. Most of the cheap and
simple inventions have, to put it bluntly, been made. . . . A benign Providence . . . has made the industry of a few large firms
an almost perfect instrument for inducing technical change.[15]

But by the 1970s it became painfully clear how imperfect Galbraith's "almost perfect instrument" had become. The inexorable
trend toward giantism had created corporations that proved, for the
most part, far too unwieldy to meet the challenges of a rapidly
changing world economy. With major firms such as DuPont and
General Electric spending as much as 90 percent of their research
funds in defense of their established lines of business, America's innovative power, once the wonder of the world, began to ebb. This
corporate "milieu of concern for tradition," notes economist Gerhard Mensch, created the conditions for a "stalemate of technology," leading to a deepening cycle of economic stagnation.[16]

To compensate for their own failings, many large firms looked toward their new acquisitions, most often companies on a faster
growth track than themselves, to supply the necessary innovative
drive. Yet after a quick spurt in earnings, most of these acquisitions
turned sour. Between 1968 and the mid-1970s conglomerate stock
prices dropped 50 percent more rapidly than other leading industrial issues while their bond prices fell almost six times the average.[17]

Nowhere was the failure of the giants more obvious than in the
great, heavily concentrated basic industries. Between 1962 and 1979
the U.S. auto industry's share of the world market dropped from
22.6 to a mere 13.9 percent; in plastics the drop was from 34.8 to 13
percent; and in railway vehicles from 34.8 to 11.6 percent. But perhaps most devastated of all was steel, once the pride of such titans as
Carnegie and Cyrus Eaton. Although the United States was a major
steel exporter as late as the 1950s, today the industry's top corporate
executives pitifully demand protection from foreign steelmakers
seeking to expand their already vast share of the American market.[18]

This industrial holocaust among large manufacturers cost American workers over half a million jobs between 1979 and 1981, virtually decimating the economies of the once immensely powerful manufacturing belt stretching from Buffalo to Chicago. But while workers lost their jobs and saw their communities devastated, the managerial aristocrats running these failing firms from glass towers far from the mills, continued to enjoy the fruits of previous glories. In 1981, as International Harvester was losing nearly $400 million a year, its chairman, Archie McCardell, was paid some $1.4 million. At United States Steel, a troubled giant in one of the nation's hardest hit industries, executive compensation for the company's chairman rose from $300,000 in 1971 to over $820,000 in 1981.[19]

These pampered executives blamed everyone but themselves for the decline of their industries. They railed against labor costs, the stock market, foreign competitors. Although Washington frequently gave them a sympathetic hearing, many of those closest to industry's problems knew clearly where the fault lay. Frank Cassel, former vice-president at Chicago-based Inland Steel, states:

> Our industry was built on the shoulders of very strong people but it became very inbred. There was little new blood. There was no incentive to improve since the big guys were all alike. They weren't two-fisted entrepreneurs. They were weak, they were followers. It boils down to that.

This failure of executive will was not an isolated phenomenon relegated to now unfashionable industries such as steel. During the 1960s and 1970s many of the most technologically sophisticated giants—RCA, General Electric, Burroughs, and Xerox—failed to keep up with the fast-paced changes in electronics, relinquishing entire markets in such products as televisions, microcomputers, and small copiers. Indeed, with notable exceptions such as IBM and Hewlett-Packard, few of the major technology-oriented giants of 1965 have maintained their positions against the competition—both foreigners and smaller domestic firms—over the ensuing fifteen years.

As Xerox and other new companies expanded, they soon displayed the same sloth and lack of focus as the older giants of basic industry. Unable to innovate quickly within their mushrooming bureaucracies, they attempted to enter new markets such as computers and word processing through the acquisition of more dynamic, smaller firms. Max Palevsky, for instance, sold his high-flying Scientific Data Systems (SDS) to Xerox in 1969 for some $900 million.[20] But Xerox's bureaucratic management mentality undermined SDS's creative thrust, causing its demise six years later. Palevsky, who resigned in disgust from Xerox's board in 1972 and subsequently started several other successful high-tech ventures, recalls:

They forgot how to stay lean and hungry. It was the way the company became. They flew first class, all those perks. A whole culture was set. It's the difference between a fast-on-your-feet company and a monopoly. At Xerox they didn't worry about profits, they just counted them. What disappeared at Xerox was opportunism. When you get to that size, you look at the world statistically. You lose the feel for the marketplace.

THE ENTREPRENEURIAL CONFIGURATION

While the managerial aristocrats at Xerox and other giants were steadily losing their "feel for the marketplace," a new generation of entrepreneurs was beginning to express theirs. In fields as diverse as computers, air packaging services, and steel, new companies were demonstrating an entrepreneurial opportunism that fundamentally altered the shape of the national economy. After nearly a century's romance with giantism, Americans in ever growing numbers are leaving the secure corporate womb and, like the pioneers described by Frederick Jackson Turner, striking out on their own for that "higher plane of existence."

Central to this new economic trend is the desire on the part of managers and, increasingly, workers, for owning equity—a piece of the action. Once thought of as all but irrelevant in the era of giant firms owned by faceless institutions and controlled by professional managers, equity has become for many businesspeople what land was to the frontiersman. Today, largely due to their access to equity, MBAs working in small business reap higher compensation after five years than their classmates working in giant firms. As the advantages of equity ownership have become more well-known, the number of companies offering worker and management ownership has mushroomed—from virtually a handful in the 1970s to some 5,000 firms with as many as 3 million workers.[21]

Nowhere has the new equity-orientation been more prevalent than in the fast-paced electronics industry. By building companies from scratch and then bringing them to the public equity market, company founders such as Televideo's Phil Huang have acquired half-billion-dollar fortunes virtually overnight. Even assembly line workers at the Los Angeles–based Tandon Corporation have reaped as much as $100,000 in profits from their company stock.

In sharp contrast to the extreme concentration of the automotive industry and other giants, the number of high-technology electronics firms has exploded as the industry has matured. Between 1965 and 1980 the number of firms in the expanding office machine and computer sector nearly tripled from 530 to over 1,470. Yet more than 80 percent of the companies in the electronics industry today have under 500 employees.[22]

Although some of the new leaders in high technology were, like Jared Anderson, products of the antiauthoritarian 1960s, many more hailed from the upper echelons of the nation's giant firms. Veteran executives such as Hal Georgens, a group vice-president with Bell & Howell, saw younger, less experienced men build new companies and amass large fortunes in the mid-1970s. The limitations of life as a salaried functionary seemed increasingly intolerable. At age 50, Georgens left his secure executive position and founded Data Electronics (DEI), a San Diego firm with annual sales now of over

$25 million. Relaxing in his modern sun-drenched office, the casually dressed Georgens recalls:

It was one of those things—either I was going to do it or I wouldn't ever. I just knew I had to be something more than twenty words in the annual report. Of course you hope to get rich but it's more than that—it's really the competitive bit.

I was bored in the big company. There was no way of evaluating your contribution. Feedback was slow. Here when I go home at night, I know what my contribution is. Feedback is instantaneous. It's a feeling of accomplishment—that's the basic kick.

To technically oriented businessmen like electrical engineer Georgens, much of "the basic kick" grows out of the creation, design, and marketing of a new product. At DEI, Georgens was able to develop an inexpensive, innovative series of disk drives with a rapidity utterly impossible at a giant like Bell & Howell. Nor could the large company hope to give him the sort of financial or psychic income for his creative contribution that became possible at his own company. The gray-haired executive says with a grin, "Here I don't have to write any memos. We just agree on the design and it happens."

The desire of the individual technologist to reap fully the fruits of his invention has played a profound role in the rise of today's entrepreneurial configuration. Contradicting the predictions of Bell and Galbraith that the new technologies would lead to the formation of an ever more hierarchical, corporate-dominated order, the revolt of the technological businessman reflects the persistence of the human factor within the science-based industries. Essentially, the academic gurus ignored the fact that engineers are also *people,* with personal goals that are often at odds with those of giant institutions.

In this regard, the new technological businessman represents but the latest chapter in the old tale of America's capitalist tinkerers—a tradition stretching from the earliest shipbuilders of New England

to Benjamin Franklin, Alexander Graham Bell, pioneer builder
James Eads, and—perhaps the greatest of all—Thomas Edison.
Driven by peculiarly personal goals, the tinkerer and the lone inventor have survived the onslaught of the Galbraithian "techno-
structure." A 1969 study of sixty-one significant 20th-century
innovations found that over half were the product of individual in-
ventors, while widely touted research labs, financed by giant business or government organizations, were responsible for only twelve.
Key contributions of the individual inventor over the last half century have included everything from air-conditioning, the automatic
transmission, and ballpoint pens to jet engines and xerography.[23]

Many of today's technological innovators have achieved success
by exploiting the discards of the corporate giants. IBM, for instance,
ignored the possibilities of the minicomputer, only to see Digital
Equipment Corporation seize the market. Similarly, it was upstart
Apple that sparked the recent boom in personal computers, after the
concept was rejected by Hewlett-Packard and other major firms.
And although they possessed the technology first, Xerox considered
the market for computer-aided transcription too small, so Oakland's
Baron Data Systems filled the gap.

In each case, the smaller firms took the initiative because an entrepreneur was able to focus employees directly toward a particular
end, avoiding the conflicts between technical, marketing, and financial staffs that are endemic in large corporations. At Redaction Office Automation, a Long Island-based firm specializing in automatic
editing components, company founder Evelyn Berezin designed and
marketed her products only after personal observation of the potential customer base, not a common practice among the CEOs of
major companies:

> If you don't go there yourself but rely on what other people tell
> you, the information is likely to be distorted or the impression
> incomplete. When you're designing a new product, you simply
> can't afford to have layers and layers of people between you
> and the eventual product users.[24]

Due largely to this lack of buffering between the different parts of the business function, small firms have been able to compensate for their relative lack of capital by using what they have more efficiently. In a 1976 study by the National Science Foundation small companies were found to produce up to twenty-four times the number of innovations per research dollar. A more recent study, conducted in 1982 by Gellman Research Associates, found small firms 2.5 times more innovative per employee than their larger counterparts.[25]

Equally important, small and medium-sized firms create a climate for innovation that almost compels larger firms to develop and introduce new technologies into the marketplace. Small firms often come up with ideas that only medium-sized or even giant companies have the wherewithal to carry out. In fact, much of the essential strength of the emerging entrepreneurial configuration lies in the interaction between organizations of different sizes, each seeking to use its peculiar scale to best advantage.

This pattern has been most prevalent within the computer industry. In 1956, the industry giant was IBM, which controlled 85 percent of the nation's computer market. Over the next two decades, however, a host of small and medium-sized companies created new technologies and such products as the personal computer that effectively halved IBM's market share. Faced with this competitive challenge, IBM has been forced to restructure itself radically and, although no longer the all-powerful monolith, it has emerged from the 1970s as perhaps the world's most dynamic giant firm. This competitive configuration, according to studies conducted by Northwestern University's F. M. Scherer, is the one best suited for promoting industrial dynamism. Scherer observes:

> All things considered, the rapid technological progress would appear to be a result of firm-size distribution which includes a preponderance of companies with sales below $200 million, pressed on one side by a horde of small, technology-oriented enterprises bubbling over with bright new ideas and on the

other a few larger corporations with the capacity to undertake exceptionally ambitious developments.[26]

Equally important, this same competitive pattern may be developing within older industries such as steel. During the 1960s and 1970s the large steel companies generally failed to modernize their operations while small "mini-mill" firms rapidly incorporated new innovations such as continuous casting and electric furnaces. Led by executives committed to steelmaking, successful "mini-mills" such as the North Carolina-based NuCor increased their share of the nation's steel market from 3 to 13 percent during the 1970s. By 1990, according to federal projections, the minis' domain could expand to as much as 25 percent. Sufficiently chastised, giant companies now talk of the "mini-mill challenge" and are hoping to implement at least some of the innovations used by NuCor and other firms like it.[27]

Perhaps nothing better illustrates the position of small and medium-sized firms on the cutting edge than their bottom-line performance. Despite the recent near hysteria about the imminent development of an information-based post-industrial economy, size has proven to be a surer guide to profits than technology. Between 1963 and 1981, for instance, publicly traded small and medium-size steel firms with capitalization under $60 million averaged an 18 percent return on equity—better than 2.5 times that of large steel companies and nearly 50 percent above those enjoyed by larger computer firms.[28]

For investors, the implications of this "small firm effect" have been profound indeed. According to one study by Professor Marc Reinganum of the University of Southern California, a dollar invested in a portfolio of companies with less than $5 million in capitalization in 1963 would have netted an investor $46 by 1980; that same dollar invested in a portfolio with companies worth over $1 billion would have produced a mere $4.[29]

Among the greatest beneficiaries of this profitable explosion among small and medium-sized firms has been a new breed of financier oriented toward the entrepreneur. The major money center banks preoccupied themselves with massive foreign loan syndications and large-scale corporate credits, but other more innovative individuals and firms assumed a major role within the entrepreneurial configuration. As small companies grew in importance, new independent state-chartered banks rose to serve their needs, tripling in number from 1976 to 1980. In much the same way asset-based lenders such as Commercial Alliance and A. J. Armstrong, also oriented to small companies, experienced a tremendous growth—particularly in equipment leasing, which exploded from $600 million in the late 1960s to well over $7 billion a decade later.[30]

But by far the most dramatic rise has been among the venture capitalists. A small, dying industry in the mid-1970s, with less than $30 million invested annually, the venture capital funds exploded to over $1.6 billion in 1982. Sparked by a reduction in the capital gains tax in 1978, these firms, often consisting of no more than three or four individuals, took enormous risks by investing in young and "start-up" companies. Although many of the investments were in high-technology firms, including such remarkable successes as Apple Computers, Prime, Televideo, and Tandon, venture funds also funded fast-growing firms in diverse fields such as uniforms, air packaging, telephone equipment, real estate, even contraceptives.[31]

In their approach to investment, most venture capitalists avoid the formula used by the majority of traditional financiers. To Stan Golder, a veteran Chicago venture capitalist who has backed new firms in fields ranging from robotics to petroleum exploration, the key to venture capital lies almost entirely with "the human factor," with the burning desire of the individual to build his own economic future. Golder, who left a top executive position at First Chicago Corporation to start his fund, recalls:

When I left the bank people thought I was crazy. The goal used to be to become the Chairman of First Chicago, GM, or Goldman Sachs. Now we've changed all that. The successes of the Tandons or the Federal Expresses have changed people's perception.

We live in a new age where people look at those models and say, "I can do that." So the guy quits his job and comes to you with an idea. You can't inject a standard budget and plan in that situation. Some people think all you need is capital to make things happen but that's not it at all. Success revolves around the character of the entrepreneur. He's the one who's going to make it happen. You can't just push a button.

AMERICA'S COMPARATIVE ADVANTAGE

This new entrepreneurial configuration, dominated by small, equity-oriented firms, represents America's best hope for preserving its world economic leadership. As the pace of technological change hastens, small and medium-sized firms provide the American economy with a unique ability to adjust to new market conditions. No other major industrialized country possesses such a storehouse of entrepreneurial energy.

Indeed, many industrial countries are increasingly concerned about their "entrepreneur gap" with the United States. While numerous American academics, politicians, and even business leaders urge the adoption of European or Japanese-style national planning, many of these same governments are actively seeking to duplicate the entrepreneurial dynamism of the United States. The government-fostered development of fledgling venture capital and small issue markets—designed to supply the equity needs of entrepreneurial firms—in many of these countries is just one indication of the powerful influence of the American model. As Jiro Tokuyama, dean of the Nomura School of Advanced Management and a highly influential Japanese economist, explains:

The entrepreneurial firms and the venture capital are the great advantages you have. These firms are creating the new changes and, as the pace of change quickens, they will become more important. In Europe and in Japan, where things are more top to bottom, change comes more slowly. If we cannot learn how to develop the entrepreneurial sector, Japan's companies will end up like the battleship *Yamato* at the end of the war, at the bottom of the Pacific.

To take full advantage of our entrepreneurial comparative advantage requires a major reordering of governmental and corporate priorities. A drastic revision of the federal tax code, creating a more advantageous tax environment for small and medium-sized firms, could facilitate greater capital formation within the dynamic, job-producing, and innovative parts of the economy. Bank regulations and practices, now oriented toward large financial institutions and their giant customers, must be changed to eliminate many of the barriers now imposed on lending to entrepreneurs. And instead of tilting toward protectionism, the American government should work to expand the ability of small, entrepreneurial firms to export their goods overseas.

To put into effect an entrepreneur-driven economic policy, however, will require a political transformation every bit as drastic as that now taking place on the economic battlefield. No matter what their contributions to society, the nation's over 15 million entrepreneurs and small businesspeople frequently find themselves virtually at war with their own government, outside the corridors of power.

For over sixty years, big business and its sister bureaucracies in labor and government have been the dominant political force in Washington. Not one President since Wilson has seriously attempted to represent the interests of independent proprietors. Even those who may have considered doing so at first have always found the voice of giant business to be ultimately more persuasive. As Mike McKevitt, Executive Director of the National Federation of Independent Business (NFIB), the nation's largest small business lobby, observes:

A mistake most administrations make . . . is that they are awed by big business in general and sort of into their deal and don't understand why it is said that . . . big business is nothing but a bunch of Argentine generals. They're awed by their uniforms and their titles.

Outranked by the "Argentine generals" of big business, the entrepreneurial sector has found itself virtually excluded from economic decision making, from the top Cabinet posts to the Federal Reserve. Even the Small Business Administration, set up in 1953 to serve the needs of the entrepreneurial constituency, has become a largely token agency without significant influence over key tax and regulatory policies. As Howard Samuels, former director of the Small Business Administration under President Lyndon Johnson and a highly successful New York entrepreneur, recalls:

> We were not a part of the decision-making process. It starts in the Executive branch and there's no access, even for the director. Policies are made in Washington but where is small business when it counts? SBA has no voice and nobody listens to it.

Perhaps nothing better illustrates the relative political impotence of small and medium-sized companies than the federal tax code. Instead of encouraging the entrepreneurs who provide new jobs and innovations, federal tax policy has been designed largely to aid those giant firms whose economic failures have punctuated the last decade. Billion-dollar companies, for instance, bear as little as one-half the income tax burden per business receipt as that levied against medium-sized firms and one-third that of small companies, according to one federal study.[32]

Even in the face of growing awareness about the importance of the entrepreneurial sector, large corporations have continued to procure huge tax advantages. In the 1981 tax reduction legislation, Congress pieced together a package including the controversial "safe harbor leasing" bill, virtually custom-made for big business. Small firms, however, received less than 13 percent of the total benefit from the multibillion-dollar tax cut, placing them at a distinct competitive disadvantage.[33]

While handing cuts to the Fortune 500 firms, Washington has been systematically imposing an ever greater share of the tax burden on job-producing small businesses. Perhaps the most onerous problem for small proprietorships has been the enormous increase in payroll taxes over the past few decades. Although it represented only 15 percent of the total federal tax picture twenty-five years ago, the payroll tax now accounts for nearly one-third of all tax revenues, placing an enormous strain on millions of labor intensive small businesses in the burgeoning service sector of the economy.

This persistent policy of malicious neglect frustrates many entrepreneurs. To Hardit Sandhu, President of Rhino Robots, a fledgling high-tech firm located on the rolling plains of Champaign, Illinois, the federal tax system seems designed to discourage his plans for further expansion. A naturalized American citizen from India, Sandhu built his company from nothing through his own personal engineering skill and business acumen. Confident of his ability to compete against the giant Japanese and American firms, Sandhu has more doubts about his ability to withstand the work of Washington:

The tax laws don't give the small man anything. All they give you is the first $100,000 in profit—you can take that and buy a screwdriver. If I could put the money I pay in taxes into the company, I could expand more. We have spent $1 million and created twenty new jobs. If General Motors spent their money like that, they could employ the whole world, but they take the loopholes and shelter the money. Yet every year we get stuck with more and more. We need incentives so we can grow, hire people, and make money, but the system seems stacked against the individual business. Sometimes it seems that our national policy is we'll pay you to sit on your ass.

2

THE ENTREPRENEUR
AND THE ESTABLISHMENT

In the winter of 1979, Bill Nourse, a slightly built, silver-haired hardware store owner from Tennessee, arrived in Washington for a meeting with leading political figures, including the President of the United States. Nourse gazed at the august trappings of power around him—the White House, Capitol Hill, the executive offices, the monotonous rows of white office buildings housing the legions of professional lobbyists who constitute this nation's real government through changing seasons and administrations.

Although he was only the representative of several hundred Southern small businessmen, Nourse was determined not to be intimidated by the purveyors or their power. After all, he reasoned, such important personages, used to dealing in multibillion-dollar appropriations, should have little trouble accepting his group's seemingly modest legislative agenda. It included a bill allowing for immediate first-year direct expenses of small capital purchases and other minor tax alterations designed to aid millions of small, increasingly hard-pressed proprietors.

What Bill Nourse soon learned was that small businessmen like himself, without the benefit of strong political organization, had lit-

tle chance of passing even the mildest reforms. Four years later, re-
calling that first Washington experience, Nourse still harbors resentment:

When I finally got to our actual proposals, everybody told me
we were wasting our time. The politicians, the lobbyists said,
"You people don't understand the process." We were rocking
the boat. They just laughed at us.

Boy, I thought I was part of the establishment. The foundation of the country. But I learned real fast that entrepreneurs
and small businessmen aren't part of that establishment in
Washington—big business gets the goodies and we get the
sugar-coated candy. I realized that the whole system was
weighted against us. It isn't a question of party politics; it's a
battle between small business and big, those who don't have
power and those who are entrenched.

This realization—that entrepreneurs and small businessmen have
been all but frozen out of the nation's power structure—has led
Nourse and thousands of other independent businessmen to co-
alesce into what might well prove the most important new political
force of the 1980s. Convinced that the entrepreneurial sector provides the best hope for solving the nation's deep-seated economic
problems, business activists are challenging the privileged status of
the nation's giant institutions in a manner not seen for over sixty
years.

Although only in its infancy, the potential of the modern entrepreneurial movement can be seen by the success of activists like
Nourse who, starting in the late 1970s, have built a network of small
business groups capable of competing in the political wars with the
well-heeled lobbies of the major corporations and other entrenched
institutions. Largely through the efforts of such groups in Tennessee,
Pennsylvania, and Massachusetts, a version of Nourse's direct ex-
pensing proposal passed through Congress in 1981, a mere two years
after the humiliations of his first fateful trip to Washington. Today,

instead of feeling awed by the Washington establishment, Nourse knows how to use it, picking up the phone to call "my Senator" or "my Congressmen"—politicians who respect the power of entrepreneurial activists. Nourse adds:

> We are making the point that we have the right to challenge every damned politician and every bill that hurts our sector of the economy. The lesson we entrepreneurs are learning is that the guys in the boardroom aren't any smarter or better because they fly around in Lear jets. The only difference is they've been there cutting the deals.

Nourse's resentment against the privileged "guys in the boardroom" reflects the experience of a businessman who battled to achieve even a modest level of success. For over a decade after leaving a secure job at General Electric, Bill Nourse made his living as an independent salesman, peddling everything from peanuts to candy throughout the small towns and cities of the mid-South.

Having finally saved enough money, he opened his Brookmeade Hardware Supply in 1975, only to discover that the store's poor location sharply limited his walk-in business. If he didn't find a market niche, he would soon be facing the abyss of bankruptcy. Then the resourceful ex-peanut salesman hit upon the idea of selling bulk orders to motel chains and apartment complexes at cut rates. Although everyone warned him that no supplier would give cut rates to an independent, Nourse persisted and eventually succeeded in breaking one of retailing's unwritten rules. By the late 1970s the twelve-hour days and seven-day weeks seemed to be paying off; Brookmeade was becoming a successful family business.

But even as sales steadily increased, Nourse discovered that for every increased profit margin, every new employee hired, the government—through taxes or imposition of paperwork—seemed to find ways of siphoning off his gains. Quickly, Nourse learned that the system provided precious few breaks for the small entrepreneur. But perhaps the most crushing blow to Nourse was a personal one.

His son, seeing his father working himself to exhaustion for what seemed to be extremely limited gains, announced he didn't want any part of the business.

It struck a nerve deep inside Bill Nourse:

> I spent a great deal of my life seeing what I had built up slipping away from my kids. Small business, to me, is more than making a living, it's really a whole way of life—whether you're starting an Apple Computer or a hardware store. The feeling of starting something is everything to me. It's something I realized I'd better try to preserve before it's too late.

For that reason, Bill Nourse spends a lot of time in airports and motels these days, crisscrossing the nation as he preaches his brand of entrepreneurial politics. Nourse's experiences with his fellow small proprietors—the shopowners, the machine shop operators, the fledgling high-tech manufacturers—convinces him that America is now poised on the brink of an "entrepreneurial rebirth," if only the necessary political pressure can be brought to bear:

> You have to go after power. That's what it's all about. We're going to keep pushing till we get an entrepreneur on the Federal Reserve, a small businessperson elected with our backing in the White House. I know it might take twenty years, but this time when we get there, we'll hold it. Main Street America will have its revolution.

A REPUBLIC OF SMALL PROPRIETORS

This overweening desire for economic self-determination, free from the constraining hand of entrenched forces, has characterized the American entrepreneurial experience from its very beginnings. Seeking to establish for themselves a new niche apart from the already controlled centers of trade and commerce, the earliest European merchants financing the first commercial ventures in North

America were ambitious outsiders—barely respectable adventurers by the standards of late medieval Europe. Those who actually took the greatest risks—the captains, pilots, and sailors—were, as Fernand Braudel has observed, "recruited from amongst the wretched classes of Europe and the world."[1]

Like the early adventurers, many of the permanent settlers to such early colonies as Virginia and Massachusetts came in search of opportunities that seemed unobtainable in the old country. As small towns and villages rose along the Atlantic coastal plain, new waves of lower- and middle-class immigrants pushed ever deeper into the fearsome interior of the new continent. There, in the woods and hills of colonial America, a new, uniquely entrepreneurial society was coming into being; in that wilderness every family's dream was to secure his own farm, blacksmith shop, or dry goods business. As Benjamin Franklin noted:

> So vast is the territory of North America that it will require many ages to settle it fully; and till it is fully settled, labor will never be cheap here, where no man continues long to labor for others.[2]

This vision of a free land "where no man continues long to labor for others" has deeply inspired Americans. Among those most animated by the independent spirit were men such as Thomas Jefferson, himself the son of a Virginia frontier farmer, who combined the values of a rough-hewn entrepreneurial society with the concepts of liberty developed by John Locke and other British philosophers.[3]

Yet even as this new democratic society was reaching out to the first wave of mountains west of the coastal plain, powerful forces in England—allied with some local landowners, merchants, and officials—imposed trade restrictions, taxation, and currency controls, driving some Americans to the brink of financial ruin and to revolution. Indeed, explaining the basic goals of the insurrection, Tom Paine stated in *Common Sense*: "Our plan is commerce."[4]

When revolution broke out in 1775, small urban proprietors along with yeoman farmers supplied much of the muscle and the blood, ultimately driving the British imperium from the colonies. For many of these small-scale entrepreneurs, the revolution represented more than a quest for independence; it was a struggle for entrepreneurial opportunity.[5]

With the withdrawal of the British from the colonies in 1783, the old British order dominated by imperial agents and landlords fell, never to rise again. But as that elite collapsed, a new one consisting of conservative plantation owners and merchants now assumed command; having dispatched the British, these interests had no intention of sharing power with the frontiersmen, farmers, and small shopkeepers who had done so much of the fighting and dying. "Those who own the country," bluntly declared New York's John Jay, "ought to govern it."[6]

Over the ensuing decades concern for the rights of these small proprietors would find their greatest champions in Thomas Jefferson and James Madison. Unlike elitists of the Federalist school such as Jay and Alexander Hamilton, these Virginia political thinkers believed that the mass of small "freeholders" represented "the safest depositories of Republican liberty."[7] To guarantee these freeholders their entrepreneurial opportunities, Jefferson, Madison, and their political heirs struggled for the continued expansion of the western frontier.

Even with the onset of industrialization in the early decades of the 19th century, America remained close to its Jeffersonian ideals. Most American manufacturers were small-scale operations, often run by former mechanics, artisans, and even shop hands. Indeed, whether it was in the booming mill towns of New England, the busy wharves of New York Harbor, or the new towns and farms of the sprawling western frontier, American capitalism of the first half of the 19th century was suffused with the spirit of continuous revolution. Any family of freemen could aspire to win its fortune and none was above the fear of losing it. Amazed by this almost breathless class mobility, a young French nobleman, Alexis de Tocqueville, observed:

After a lapse of a little more than sixty years, the aspect of society is totally altered; the families of the great landed proprietors are almost all co-mingled with the general mass. . . . The last trace of hereditary ranks and distinctions is destroyed; the law of partition has reduced all to one level.[8]

Yet this very pattern of rapid economic and social change, so impressive to a European like de Tocqueville, disturbed some of the entrenched forces that had played a major part in the revolutionary period. By the time Andrew Jackson and his rough-edged frontier supporters gained the Presidency in the 1830s, the influence of the old New England and Philadelphia mercantile families was already well on the wane. In their place the new entrepreneurial forces, including the ascendant Wall Street banking community, the frontier capitalists of the West, and the industrialists of the Northeast, clearly emerged as the leading factors in the nation's economic life.

The other major power group left over from the 1776 revolution, the slave-owners of the South, proved a far more intractable problem for these new business leaders.[9] By the 1850s it had become increasingly clear that these two Americas—the free, industrializing society of the North and West and the plantation-oriented, semifeudal South—would become locked in an irrepressible conflict. When that conflict exploded into the great Civil War, the new industrialism slew the last vestiges of Europe's feudal past on American soil. Gone forever was what poet Stephen Vincent Benét would later call the South's "purple dream":

Of the America we have not been,
The tropic empire, seeking the warm sea,
The last foray of aristocracy . . .[10]

FROM MOGULS TO MANAGERS

With the planter elite crushed, America's triumphant industrial entrepreneurs now forged ahead with unprecedented vigor. In the fifty years following the Civil War, America's industrial production doubled every fifteen years, surpassing not only that of its traditional rival Great Britain but of the entire European continent. By 1910, in virtually every major category of enterprise from agriculture and steel to textiles and electricity, America had emerged as the number one force on the face of the earth.[11]

Yet to a great extent, this remarkable progress came at the expense of the same small proprietors who had been so responsible for the beginnings of American industrialism. Between the 1880s and 1904 there were over 318 major consolidations, affecting over 80 percent of the nation's existing manufacturing industries.[12]

Ironically, many of the architects of this new industrial system came from backgrounds remarkably similar to those small proprietors whose enterprises they so often decimated; few inherited more than a tiny part of the empires they eventually created. In this era, it was possible for a man like Thomas Mellon, the son of an immigrant Ulster farmer from western Pennsylvania, to build an empire that would spawn a brood of giants including Mellon Bank, Gulf Oil, and Alcoa. John D. Rockefeller, perhaps the greatest and certainly the most hated of the men later to be known as "the moguls," came from a background even less respectable; his father was a failed purveyor of snake oil remedies from upstate New York.[13]

As they reached the very heights of success, such self-made entrepreneurs as steel baron Andrew Carnegie, immigrant son of an impoverished Scottish weaver, came to regard themselves as the natural rulers of the American economy. Drawing heavily on the social Darwinism of British philosopher Herbert Spencer, Carnegie was convinced "the laws of nature" sanctified his ascent to industrial supremacy, albeit on the backs of his competitors and workers.[14]

Fearful of extinction before the onslaught of the giant interests, many of the remaining independent proprietors rallied around the Populist movement in the 1880s. Particularly strong in the South and West, the Populists reflected, in the words of historian Richard Hofstadter, an "entrepreneurial radicalism" fighting to protect the independent proprietor from the depredations of the giant industrial trusts, railroads, and banks. At the same time that the Populists upheld the Jeffersonian belief in small proprietors, they turned away sharply from the laissez-faire ideology of the 18th century, seeing in government the last hope of curbing the power of giant interests.[15]

Similarly, entrepreneurs in other states played a central role in the formation of the Progressive movement which, like the Populist, sought to curb the overweening power of the trusts. Business leaders such as California's Rudolph Spreckels and Harris Weinstock helped spearhead the Progressive effort against the monopolistic pretensions of the "Octopus," the Southern Pacific. Other entrepreneurs assuming major roles in the Progressive movement included Illinois Governor John Altgeld, Michigan Governor Hazen Pingree, and Sam "Golden Rule" Jones, the mayor of Toledo.[16]

Pressing their campaign against the strong opposition of the entrenched interests, the Populists and the Progressives managed to correct some of the most glaring abuses of the corporate giants. Under President Theodore Roosevelt and his successor William Howard Taft, significant antitrust actions were taken for the first time against such giant firms as Standard Oil and the American Tobacco Company. Under Democrat Woodrow Wilson's "New Freedom," new regulatory bodies such as the Federal Trade Commission and the Clayton Antitrust Act imposed tough restrictions on the trusts' use of "unfair competition" against the small and medium-sized firms.[17]

Yet despite these successes, small proprietors failed over the long haul to regain the degree of political power they had exercised in the first half of the 19th century. The superior organization of the great industrial and financial interests blunted many of Wilson's reform initiatives. By the end of his administration entrepreneurial radicalism had fallen into an historical eclipse from which it is only now slowly recovering. World War I and the 1917 Bolshevik revolution had weakened the reformist impulse among entrepreneurs. Seeking to bathe themselves in the soothing elixir of normalcy, small businessmen accepted the slogan "the business twins—big and small" and seemed ready to surrender their right to political and, ultimately, economic determination.[18]

More than any single factor, the unprecedented prosperity of the

1920s did the most to squelch the fires of entrepreneurial radicalism. Many small firms enjoyed the boom in the urbanized areas, where new skyscrapers and monster factories rose like monuments to a bracing new era of industrial progress. So spectacular seemed their accomplishments that many Americans not only abandoned any thought of restraining the major corporations but actually believed that they alone could solve virtually all the nation's problems. Asked *Life* magazine: "Are we approaching a millennium in which the job of running the world will slip away from obtrusive politicians and be taken over by men trained in the shop?

THE MANAGERIAL ARISTOCRACY

The prime architects of this new industrial millennium stood in sharp contrast to the entrepreneurial buccaneers of the previous century. Although they frequently built upon foundations laid by the moguls, the new leaders were essentially corporate civil servants, sophisticated, university-trained members of what Pitirim Sorokin would later describe as "the managerial aristocracy." These "systems men," often working with the monied heirs of the moguls, established a hegemony over American business that has persisted to the current day.

Eager to distinguish themselves from their swashbuckling forebears, the new managerial elite took elaborate steps to reconcile the new form of bureaucratic capitalism with public-spiritedness. In this effort, they found their ultimate advocate in Herbert Hoover, who sought to foster a society dominated by giant, albeit benign, industrial empires. Hoover urged the end of "arbitrary individual ownership" and "the great wastes of over-reckless competition."[19]

In his celebration of the virtues of bigness and cooperation, Hoover reflected the views of a society growing accustomed to giant scale. By the end of the 1920s, fully 38 percent of the nation's business wealth, outside of banks, was in the hands of some 200 giant corporations. And although the number of small firms continued to grow, their share of total employment sank to a mere quarter of the working population by 1929.[20]

The Depression further accelerated the trend toward giantism in the person of Franklin Roosevelt. Many top corporate leaders hoped for a realist capable of dealing with the economic crisis without interfering with privileged positions. Originally a Progressive with strong Jeffersonian leanings, Roosevelt later came to believe that the era of the entrepreneur had ended and that America now had to face "the soberer, less dramatic business of administering resources and plants already in hand."[21]

This approach impressed many top corporate executives, among them General Electric's Gerard Swope who, working with the New Dealers and other leading executives, laid down the foundation for what veteran small business advocate Walter Stults has characterized as a "coalition of the bigs"—big government, big business, and big labor—whose members would determine the parameters of economic policy.

Abandoned by the powerbrokers of both parties, the independent proprietors were reduced largely to playing a peripheral role in national political life. Small business would pay mightily for its exclusion from this new coalition, both during the New Deal and its aftermath. Although the number of small businesses continued to increase steadily, often because proprietors had nowhere else to go, big corporations took increasing advantage of government policies to gobble up ever larger chunks of key industries. In the years before the New Deal the top 316 manufacturing firms held 35 percent of the industrial working capital assets; by 1938 their share had mushroomed to 47 percent.[22]

This process of consolidation received a further boost with the onset of World War II. "Risk-free war capitalism," historian Kim McQuaid has observed, "poured a river of federal dollars into parched corporate treasuries . . . [to] produce profound changes in the structure of the American economy."[23]

At the heart of this new symbiosis between giant business and increasingly mammoth government stood the Reconstruction Finance Corporation (RFC), whose revival some corporate leaders and public policy enthusiasts still seek today. In the first thirteen years following its founding by President Hoover in 1932, the RFC spent over $35 billion, most of it in the form of loans or investments in large banks, railroads, and industrial giants, saving not a few from extinction.

As the nation readied for war in 1940, the RFC steered most of the billions in federal contracts to giant companies, even though as many as one-third of the smaller defense-oriented plants could have taken up the slack at lower cost, according to one Commerce Department survey. As a result of this pro-big business tilt the percentage of contracts held by giant companies jumped from 30 percent to over 70 percent between 1940 and 1943. Even after the war, less than one quarter of the RFC's loans went to borrowers of under $50,000.[24]

Ultimately, the corruption bred by its unprecedented power led to the agency's demise. President Roosevelt himself had been asked to intervene in the RFC's affairs and actually tried to convince RFC administrator Jesse Jones to make low-cost loans to such influential political allies as publishers David Stern of the *Philadelphia Record* and George Ford Milton of the *Chattanooga News*. While the principled and savvy Jones managed to turn from temptation, the same cannot be said for his successors.[25]

By the late 1940s it became well-known that RFC loans could be had if one went through the right operative at the Democratic National Committee or the properly placed Washington attorney. One young Missouri man, for instance, with connections to the Truman White House, used his influence at the RFC to rise from a $1,080-a-year government messenger to earning well over $40,000 by serving as a middleman in dealings with RFC-financed corporations. The corruption festered until 1953, when the agency was finally abolished.

Although the RFC ended in disgrace, the marriage between the public and private managerial elites successfully survived the New Deal. In such groups as the Committee for Economic Development and the Business Council, the leaders of the two dominant sectors could meet and shape the policies of the corporate state outside the hurly-burly of conventional politics. After the death of Roosevelt, this liaison grew even closer.

Indeed, by mid-century many prominent Americans, liberal intellectuals as well as conservative business leaders, fully embraced the gospel of giantism. With the nation's economy now producing almost one-half of the world's industrial output, widely respected leaders such as Tennessee Valley administrator David Lilienthal saw in America's success the affirmation of the new ethos. Urging the nation to abandon its Jeffersonian roots, Lilienthal observed:

As a nation we can't live in a world of economic folk dancing and basket-weaving and simultaneously in the world of the big productive machine. . . . Our productive and distributive superiority, our fruitfulness, rest upon bigness. Size is our greatest single asset.[26]

THE ENTREPRENEURIAL ROAD HOME

Although disdained by the intellectual and political elite, small business during the post-war years once again took to the political struggle. Many, embittered by the New Deal experience, sympathized with the political right wing and such leaders as Senator Joseph McCarthy, who appealed to their concerns about an America slipping away from the familiar ideals of Main Street.

But, at the same time, new small business groups, such as the National Federation of Independent Business (NFIB) and the Conference of Small Business Organizations, continued to fight for some of the policies once sought by the Populists and the Progressives. Although badly outgunned in Congress, these groups helped push the passage of such key antimonopoly legislation as the Celler-O'Mahoney-Kefauver Act of 1949 and the strengthening of the antimerger provisions of the Clayton Antitrust Act in 1950. Other major accomplishments of this era included the formation of a permanent Senate Small Business Committee and the establishment of the Small Business Administration in 1953.[27]

Despite these triumphs, the influence of NFIB and other entrepreneurial lobbies remained extremely limited throughout the

1950s. Dwight Eisenhower's Republican administration, although less responsive to big labor, proved almost comically subservient to the interests of the managerial aristocracy. So deep-seated was the administration's commitment to giantism that it simply could not differentiate between corporate needs and those of the nation. As Charles Wilson, Eisenhower's Defense Secretary and former head of General Motors put it: "What is good for the United States is good for the General Motors Corporation and vice versa."[28]

Nor did political conditions improve markedly for entrepreneurs when the Democrats, under John Kennedy and then Lyndon B. Johnson, captured the White House. The "best and the brightest"—the gifted Ivy League–trained public servants brought to Washington during the glamorous days of "Camelot"—proved even less responsive to the needs of entrepreneurs than their plodding Republican predecessors. Kennedy might have been more willing than Eisenhower to take on corporate chieftains such as U.S. Steel's Roger Blough, but his "conservative Keynesian" economic policies were largely designed to win the confidence of most major business leaders.[29] His economic policy in general reflected the almost total abandonment of the entrepreneur by the liberal and corporate establishments. Dismissing the old concerns about corporate concentration, Kennedy saw economics as consisting essentially of "technical problems," solvable only by the close cooperation of both corporate and governmental experts. In this new technocratic equation, John Kenneth Galbraith would later write, the entrepreneur could be confidently dismissed as "a diminishing figure in the industrial system."[30]

Yet precisely as Galbraith was prophesying his ultimate demise, the entrepreneur was already staging an historic comeback on the national economic scene. Between 1950 and 1970, the number of new business incorporations jumped from under 100,000 to over 300,000 annually. More importantly, some of these new firms were suddenly outperforming and taking market share away from the supposedly impregnable giants in such key fields as electronics and steel.

Nowhere was this resurgence of the entrepreneurial spirit more profound than in the Sunbelt—the string of states stretching from North Carolina to California. There, far from the academies of Harvard and the corporate offices of Manhattan, new empires were being built at a rate not seen since the age of the moguls. Many entrepreneurial parvenus such as H. L. Hunt, Henry Salvatori, and Clint Murchison emerged from the oil fields with fortunes far in excess of those enjoyed by managers of eastern corporate giants. Others seized the technological initiative and built empires in the new electronics-based aerospace industry; they included Howard Hughes, James Ling of Dallas's LTV, and Litton Industries founder Tex Thornton.

Frequently, like Andrew Carnegie before them, these new entrepreneurial giants looked with contempt upon the polished boardroom politicians who dominated the government-sponsored Business Council and other outposts of the "managerial aristocracy." To them, the eastern business elite seemed almost devoid of the capitalist zeal so characteristic of its mogul forebears. As Tex Thornton, the product of an impoverished west Texas upbringing, saw it:

> That guilt feeling is what kills the guys back east. Maybe they feel for what the robber barons did, but hell, there shouldn't be guilt for building things, making money. I created 80,000 jobs—people benefit from what we do. I feel wholesome about it. Those rich easterners, a lot haven't worked, never created a job for anyone, never did anything new. If you've got wealth and haven't earned it, you don't feel wholesome about it. I'd feel guilty too if I were them.

By the early 1960s Thornton and other Sunbelt businessmen felt themselves strong enough to take on the "rich easterners." For Sunbelt entrepreneurs such as California oilman Henry Salvatori, Barry Goldwater's presidential campaign provided an opportunity to crusade for the restoration of "old-fashioned primitive capitalism," a message that appealed not only to the new rich but to thousands of aspiring entrepreneurs across the country. Like them, Goldwater suspected that big businessmen were far too willing to accept the social controls and bureaucratic compromises of the Galbraithian industrial state. The Arizona senator, himself the son of pioneer capitalists, lamented the passing of "the old leader of business, the man who would stand and scrap for what he knew was right for his business and the country."[31]

Although Goldwater's 1964 campaign went down to humiliating defeat, many of the same Sunbelt entrepreneurial forces continued their drive to unseat the old eastern elite. In 1968, with the election of Richard Nixon, they won a partial victory; Nixon, a Californian, had strong ties both with the entrepreneurial Goldwater constituency and with the mainstream of corporate America. Yet deep inside, Nixon remained a political outsider, suspicious of the old-line corporate leadership from the Fortune 500 companies. "The American leader class has really had it in terms of their ability to lead," Nixon wrote in 1972. "It's sickening to have to receive them at the White House as I often do and to hear them whine and whimper. . . ."[32]

Whether or not they planned it, as Kirkpatrick Sale and others have suggested, Watergate relieved "the leader class" from the task of dealing with Richard Nixon. Under Gerald Ford and to some extent Jimmy Carter, the old forces of the business establishment enjoyed a somewhat more congenial environment. Although Carter, himself the owner of a small peanut warehouse, ran a mildly populist presidential campaign, in office he made a determined attempt to win over big business leaders, most of whom had preferred the rather pliable Ford. As his administration began to sink, Carter's need for the establishment's support grew increasingly desperate. In the end, the man who had promised to "turn the government of this country inside out"[33] presided over an administration dominated by the very forces that had held a stranglehold on national political power. As Lewis A. Shattuck, a veteran small business activist and executive vice-president of the 1500-member Smaller Business Association of New England, observes:

Nobody seemed to have a better appreciation of small business than Carter, at first. He had a small business issues desk in his campaign and that was a first. He seemed to want to do a lot for us. . . . But he ended being with big business. They charmed the pants off him. For a small peanut farmer from South Georgia, the guys from Citibank must have seemed awfully impressive.

Much of the credit for Carter's drift toward big business belonged to the managerial aristocracy's new club, the Business Roundtable. Founded in the early 1970s through the insistence of Roger Blough, former chairman of U.S. Steel, the Roundtable was an association of over 150 top officials from the ranks of the Fortune 500 giants. By 1976 *Business Week* described it as "the most powerful voice in business." Working behind the scenes, the Roundtable developed the reputation, according to Ralph Nader's Congresswatch, as "the most effective invisible lobby on Capitol Hill." Through direct meetings with President Carter, such Roundtable leaders as Irving Shapiro of DuPont, Reginald Jones of General Electric, and John deButts of AT&T became the President's "business brain trust" without even having to pledge their political support. Members of the Roundtable, by the very size of the institutions they represented, considered themselves the supreme spokesmen for the American business community.

But by the late 1970s, this divine right of the corporate titans to speak for the American business community was being challenged sharply by the ever-swelling ranks of entrepreneurs and small proprietors. After decades of steady growth, the Fortune 500 companies had simply ceased to compete effectively in world markets or to produce new innovations or new jobs; that role, increasingly, fell to the small and medium-sized firms, particularly in the burgeoning high-technology area. Emboldened by the travails of such giants as Chrysler and International Harvester, entrepreneurs were beginning to feel that they, not the declining dinosaurs of the boardroom, should assume the mantle of business leadership. In the words of George Hatsopoulous, founder of Thermo-Electron, a Massachusetts-based high-technology firm:

The big guns have no credibility anymore. We are the only hope left in this country. The big companies have thrown up their hands in the battle and surrendered. Now it's up to the small and mid-sized companies to take over leadership and educate both the Congress and the public.

Unlike the Goldwaterites of the mid-1960s, however, Hatsopoulos and other activists in recent years have largely eschewed the right-wing rhetoric characteristic of many entrepreneurs since the New Deal. As the entrepreneurial community has grown, it has become increasingly diverse in its politics. Former Berkeley radicals, seeking "personal self-determination" through independent business, and right-wing conservatives have found a way to work together on issues of mutual concern to their businesses.

This new entrepreneurial politics first emerged in 1977 during the campaign to reduce the capital gains tax. Doubled in 1969, the high capital gains rate was severely choking the flow of venture funds to young high-technology firms locked in a bitter competitive battle with Japan. Increasingly desperate, a small coalition of entrepreneurial groups launched an all-out effort to reduce the tax.

Led by the American Electronics Association (AEA), a high-technology industry group two-thirds of whose member companies have less than 200 employees, and then AEA Chairman Edward Zschau, the capital gains measure was successfully pushed through in 1978. Although big business ultimately got behind the bill, it was clear that the small business allies had chosen the issue and spearheaded its passage. With the tax reduced, the flow of venture capital broke the $1 billion mark by the early 1980s.[34]

Since their 1978 triumph, small and medium-sized companies have intensified their political pressure. A great boost came from the 1980 White House Conference on Small Business, which resulted in a more united, better organized small business community. New leaders such as Bill Nourse of Tennessee now rose to the fore, joining other well-established groups.

In 1981 the Conference's chairman, American Stock Exchange

Chairman Arthur Levitt, pieced together another new and powerful entrepreneurial group, the American Business Conference (ABC), a coalition of eighty-five fast-growing medium-sized ($25 million to $1 billion in sales) companies. Within less than two years, the ABC has mounted a strong, increasingly effective challenge to the Roundtable and other representatives of the Fortune 500. Citing the widening gap in economic performance between the entrepreneurial and big business sectors, ABC President Jack Albertine believes the young, emerging companies are destined to succeed the leviathans as America's business leaders:

> The corporate bureaucrats are interested only in retaining their earnings and big salaries while our guys are into equity and expansion. It's basically boiling down to a question of perspective and power. Over time, I think it will become clear that the balance of power is shifting away from those big old companies and toward us.

Yet despite the success of such groups as ABC, entrepreneurs still have a long way to go before they can reverse the decades-long drift toward the giants. The enactment in 1981 of such Roundtable-backed legislation as the "safe-harbor leasing" bill proved the resiliency of big business's lobbying power. Similarly, pressures for increased protectionism, favored by auto, steel, and other giant companies, continue to gain support in Washington despite their generally negative effects on small and medium-sized firms.

This conflict between entrepreneurs and the established forces—so much a part of our national experience—can be expected to grow in the coming years. Indeed, even such traditionally conservative groups as the NFIB are preparing for increased conflict with the well-funded, well-organized "old boy network" whose influence seems to find its way into every White House. "We are going to have to fight for everything we get," remarks NFIB research director Denny Dennis.

The amassed power of the "bigs" notwithstanding, Dennis and

other entrepreneurial activists believe the nation is ready to end its century-old affair with giantism and return to its entrepreneurial roots. "You know, we entrepreneurs have one real advantage over everyone else—we're too dumb to know what's impossible," asserts former AEA chairman Zschau, now Congressman from California's Silicon Valley. "We are people who have succeeded because we didn't know we could fail. We have spent our lives being told the things we wanted to do were impossible but we've always found a way to make it happen."

3

MAKING IT AS AN OUTSIDER

In 1965, a thin, nervous 21-year-old with mahogany hair left the security and comfort of her small town in Germany's Ruhr Valley for San Francisco. Drawn by the region's social ferment, with its questioning of established values, Lore Harp came to the Bay area and lived like a "flower child." The future computer industry entrepreneur washed dishes, cleaned houses, and worked at odd jobs. Yet even as she was down to her last thirty dollars, Harp retained an irrepressible self-confidence that someday in California she would build a future for herself, on her own terms.

Lore Harp's road to economic independence was a circuitous one. Not long after arriving in California, she met a bright young engineer named Bob Harp. They were soon married and, with the Vietnam-induced aerospace boom at full tilt, Bob found a lucrative job at Hughes Aircraft in Los Angeles. They bought a home in the sprawling San Fernando Valley suburbs north of the city, had two children, and lived what seemed like a late 1960s version of Ozzie and Harriet.

Soon bored by her domestic lifestyle, Lore Harp decided to go into business. In 1976 she teamed up with another restless soul, a former New York stockbroker named Carole Ely. At first they toyed with the idea of starting a travel agency. But then Bob Harp's work with computers suggested the idea of supplying circuit boards to computer hobbyists, a group just then developing beyond the cult stage. With $6,000 garnered from family savings and some circuit designs from Bob Harp, the two housewives began Vector Graphics as a cottage factory, assembling computer kits in Harp's suburban kitchen.

As their market grew—the "weirdo" hobbyists, Harp recalls, "drooled" over the powerful homemade kits—Vector Graphics ran into cash-flow problems. Looking for a regular source of credit to tide them over between customer payments, Harp and Ely visited their local branch banks. Relaxing today in her secluded home by an artificial lake, Harp reminisces:

> We went there thinking we had something to offer, but we were naive. I went to every one of them and they wouldn't give us anything. They didn't like the risks. To them we were just a couple of housewives who didn't know anything. They didn't think there was much of a market for what we were doing.

Turned down by the banks, Harp scrambled to keep Vector afloat. Not only were orders increasing, but a new type of customer, more interested in business applications, was beginning to show interest in the low-cost computer kits. Yet even as she searched for financial backing, Harp was forced to stave off the bill collectors. She invited company reps into her kitchen, gave them coffee, and persuaded them to extend her credit another few days. "The older guys saw me as a little protégée, they wanted to be nice to me because I was a woman," Harp remembers. "It used to bother me, but I realized I wasn't going to change them, so now I take advantage of them."

By serving their customers and slowly improving their product line, Harp and Ely began to build Vector into a substantial company. Soon the cash flow began to improve, and by 1978 sales topped $2 million. Convinced they were poised for a breakthrough, Harp started searching out money for a massive expansion into the burgeoning business computer market. Still pulling only $18,000 a year in salary, she went out in full pursuit of the high-stakes rollers of California's tough-minded venture capital community.

At the end of 1978, Harp met someone willing to take Vector Graphics seriously. A refugee from the comparatively staid climate of Europe, Jean Deleage was intrigued enough to invite Harp to a meeting at his San Francisco office. After discussing her expansion plans for two hours, Harp had won not only the soft-spoken Frenchman's respect but her first half million in venture financing.

By 1982, Vector had emerged as a power in the highly competitive desk-top market, with over 400 employees and sales of over $36 million. At the same time, however, some of the nation's most powerful companies, including IBM, were making a determined push into Vector's small business computer market.

Faced with increasing competition and a severe economic downturn, Vector's sales took a nosedive, and in the spring of 1983 Harp announced losses of over $1.3 million. Steeling herself, Harp restructured her company, upgraded its product line, and honed its strategy. She was determined not to let go of her personal dream:

I just want to do what I want to do—that's why I came to this country in the first place. Everything in life is ego. You are never removed from that. It's an extension of your dreams, of having control, of saying something and having it done. There's only so much material gain you can get out of it. It comes down to self-fulfillment and creating fulfillment for others. It's being able to do a totally personal thing. All I want to do is live an interesting life. The curiosity factor is key. You want to keep pushing out, keep growing. When you're green you grow, when you're ripe, you rot.

LIFE ON THE CUTTING EDGE

Determined outsiders like Lore Harp, undeterred by social conventions, have done much to turn California into the advanced station for America's new entrepreneurial economy. No other state so bustles with restless spirits, new companies, new ideas. In virtually every industrial vanguard, from space and computers to telecommunications and biotechnology, California is the world's unquestioned leader. Nearly one-quarter of the nation's high-technology electronics firms—almost four times more than nearest rival Texas—are located within the Golden State. Four of the five fastest growing small publicly-owned firms on *Inc.* magazine's 1983 100-List and twenty of the top 100 (more than twice the number from any other state) are based in California. For years, the state has been among the leaders in new business formations; between 1975 and 1979 the rate of business starts was double the national average.[1]

Many factors have contributed to this great entrepreneurial surge. The nation's finest public university, along with such exceptional private institutions as California Institute of Technology and Stanford University, have certainly played a major part. So, too, have the state's great physical resources—its snow-rich mountains, fertile soil, temperate climate. But even these explanations do not get to the heart of the California experience, the almost fanatically individualist spirit animating its history from the days of the Gold Rush to the current high-technology explosion. Hank Riggs, Professor of Industrial Engineering at Stanford, former Vice-President of Memorex Corporation and now a member of the board of directors of six small high-tech firms, observes:

> The single biggest piece of folklore is that Stanford created Silicon Valley. It really was the atmosphere, the cultural climate that did it. Most of the high-tech companies didn't come out of Stanford. . . . Silicon Valley is really a social and cultural phenomenon. It has to do with risk-taking, an acceptance of failure and change being at the core of that culture. That's why it happened here and not in Cleveland. It's the lack of societal pressure, nobody caring what they think at the country club.

California's virulently entrepreneurial culture, like that of the rest of the country, was formed in the crucible of its frontier experience.

Isolated from the centers of political and cultural power, California served as a beacon to ambitious outsiders and parvenus, from Gold Rush robber baron Mark Hopkins to agribusinessman Henry Miller to Bank of America founder A. P. Giannini.

Like Lore Harp, many of these intrepid entrepreneurs entered business without the credentials thought necessary in the established business centers of Europe and the Atlantic seaboard. California soon became a land where "pirates" could take on the airs of gentry and even the poorest boy could dream of building an empire in the vast, exotic land. As novelist Hamlin Garland would later write:

> Whenever the conditions of his native place pressed too hard upon him, the artisan or the farmer has turned his face towards the prairies and forests of the West. . . . Thus before the days of '49, the West had become the Golden West, the land of wealth and freedom and happiness. All of the associations called upon by the spoken word, the West, were fabulous, mythic, hopeful.[2]

The great gold finds of 1849 transformed California almost over-night into a battleground for capitalist passions. Lured by the chimera of easy money, the state's population surged from 15,000 in 1848 to 165,000 two years later, doubling again within the next decade.[3] Arriving at the great port city of San Francisco, ships bearing the adventurers of the world—Chilean miners, French prostitutes, Chinese merchants and coolies, German workmen, Yankee entrepreneurs—disgorged their human cargo, the first seekers of the California dream.

Like the early settlers of the Atlantic Coast, most of the new migrants hailed from the lower orders of society. While the vast majority of the great eastern capitalists of the late 19th century came from upper- or middle-class backgrounds, almost half of all successful western mining entrepreneurs were of distinctly lower-class origins. "In this Western country," wrote Colorado mining magnate Irving Howbert, "there are singularly few men who have accomplished great success for themselves, who have been swathed during the formative period of their lives in the enervating folds of luxury."[4]

Risk dominated the business outlooks of many of the early western entrepreneurs. In virtually all the industries of pre-World War II California, from agriculture to mining to movies, fortunes were regularly made and lost overnight. This helped produce a gambling mentality among California capitalists. To self-made, self-trained entrepreneurs such as mining engineer Dennis Riordan, boom and bust were simply natural parts of the same system, something one accepted with the best possible humor. In 1917, after a lifetime in the mines of the West, the Irish immigrant, then well into his sixties, commented:

> In a small way I was always willing and ready to take chances, and have been broke and flush perhaps twenty times, and expect to be broke again before I pass in my checks.[5]

As part of this risk-taking mentality, California entrepreneurs developed a particularly hedonistic approach to business. Whereas the Atlantic and Midwestern businessmen tended to adopt the class-oriented, staid forms of European capitalism, California emerged as the playground of the brash, occasionally irresponsible economic adventurer. This peculiar atmosphere of freedom, attractive to all sorts of cults and other bizarre social manifestations, also made California a fertile ground for such untested new industries as motion pictures, aircraft, and branch banking in the years before World War II.

Equally important, the state's relative lack of fixed social classes opened the door for ethnic minorities and parvenus often ignored in the more settled business communities of the East. The leaders of California agriculture, such as German immigrant Henry Miller, rarely came from well-heeled backgrounds. Similarly, the giants of California banking, from vegetable merchant Amadeo Giannini to today's venture capitalists, hardly fit the button-down mold of bankers on Wall Street or Chicago's Loop, and the founding fathers of Hollywood, from William Fox to Jesse Lasky, hailed mostly from the slums of the Northeast or the ghettos of Europe. "The guys here have always had a 'go to hell' attitude," observes Dave Norris, a former executive with Kaiser Industries and now a Los Angeles management consultant. "There's not much class consciousness in the Los Angeles business community. The social registry of this town is about one step removed from the bandits."

Perhaps no figure epitomized California's unique entrepreneurial culture more than Howard Hughes, the Texas millionaire whose vision laid the foundation for the state's ascendancy in aerospace and high-technology electronics. When he started building his empire in the 1930s, few members of the entrenched eastern elite took him seriously, dismissing him as an ill-behaved nouveau riche Texan gone Hollywood. Even as late as the early 1940s, top eastern engineers and scientists at Harvard and MIT chided their California colleagues for working with Hughes's "little fly-by-night operation."[6]

Yet over the next ten years that "fly-by-night operation" would develop into the nerve center of the world's most advanced aerospace complex. Drawn to its loose lifestyle and reputation for technological daring, engineers, technicians, scientists, and other professionals converged upon California, increasing by 200 percent between the 1940s and the 1970s, five times the rate for the eastern states.[7] As Charles Thornton, a top Hughes aide and later founder of Litton Industries, recalls:

> Here you were not bound by tradition. You could approach things with freshness, to start anew. . . . You could put together new products, new equipment, new concepts. It's the go-west-young-man thing. It's exploring new territory. . . . It would have been a lot less satisfying to work in some big eastern company. We Californians are simply a more enterprising people. People come here for opportunities, the whole underlying theme of California is one of individual responsibility.

Although Litton itself became a massive corporate bureaucracy with sales well over $4.5 billion, it did not turn into the sort of self-contained, paternalistic corporate organism so dominant in the East and Midwest. Like Thornton, many of those who came to work at Litton possessed big entrepreneurial dreams of their own; over twenty-seven of the company's executives have founded or taken over other firms.[8] When aerospace employment dropped 25 percent at the close of the Vietnam war in the mid-1970s, technological entrepreneurs from Litton and other defense-related firms led the rapid transformation of the state's high-technology industries into their consumer product orientation.

These young high-technology companies—with a rate of job creation some forty-six times that of mature firms in the industry[9]—more than made up for the job losses suffered from defense-related cutbacks. Between 1975 and 1979, well before the Reagan military buildup, California's high-technology employment jumped from 420,000 to over 574,000, well over four times the growth rate enjoyed by states such as Illinois and New York, although each possessed ample educational and financial resources to sustain high-technology growth.[10] Roger Altman, managing director of Wall Street's Lehman Brothers investment firm, points out:

> The thing that differentiates our people from the California entrepreneurs is that those guys are hungry, they have this drive. I can get the guys who work in the high-technology companies at 7:00. Try to reach the officer of a Fortune 500 company here after 5:00, forget it. . . . People in this environment sign on for security, they are risk-averse, and they just expect things to come to them. These people have all sorts of opportunities, but very few of them want to take a risk. They wouldn't work at Vector Graphics because it might get acquired in five years, it's not big enough. It's a corporate mind-set and that's what makes New York different from California.

THE EFFICIENT HEDONISTS

Unwilling to accept the "corporate mind-set," California's high-technology entrepreneurs are creating a new capitalist culture capable of propelling the American economy into the coming century. In Silicon Valley, the nation's leading high-technology center, few firms ever achieve giant scale. Only one, Hewlett-Packard, stands among the nation's hundred largest industrial corporations, while more than 80 percent of the Valley's firms have less than 200 employees.[11]

Central to the small-is-better culture of the Valley and other high-technology areas of California has been the ample supply of entrepreneurial role models. By the 1970s, over twenty-one companies had developed from the single example set by Fairchild Semiconductors, all led by California technologists frustrated with the East Coast-controlled companies. These included such future giants as Intel, National Semiconductor, and Advanced Micro-Devices. So relentless is the desire for economic self-determination in Silicon Valley that attempts by the bigger firms to cut back on spin-offs through stock options and smaller work units have largely failed; one study even found that such attempts to compensate for bigness only encouraged executives to break ranks and strike out on their own.[12]

In the pattern established by William Randolph Hearst, Howard Hughes, and other California entrepreneurs, the high-tech leaders behave in ways sometimes shocking to those used to the muted tones of the big corporate boardroom. Advanced Micro-Devices founder Jerry Sanders, for instance, engages in what amounts to an almost reckless display of wealth, from his several Rolls-Royces to his estate in the pricey Bel-Air section of Los Angeles. Dressed in the height of Italian fashion, Sanders, one business associate jokes, "always looks like he just got off the plane from Las Vegas." Yet behind the glitzy facade, Sanders' unconventionality expresses a certain entrepreneurial joie de vivre rarely seen among the gray-clad men of the managerial elite. Sanders, a product of working-class Polish parents from Chicago, says pointedly: "I don't think they enjoy their wealth, but I do."[13]

Although not every high-tech millionaire is as flashy as Sanders, the "captains outrageous" of Silicon Valley share a healthy disdain for the traditional folkways of eastern corporations. To most of them, work itself is the ultimate source of hedonistic pleasure, not an expression of any long-term obligation to either God or man, as suggested by some latter-day moralists. Indeed, some top high-techers regard the essential elements of the old-line corporate culture—noblesse oblige, class distinction, hierarchical business relations, exclusive clubs—as almost comically archaic. James Treybig, founder of Tandem Computers, a fast-growing firm with over $312 million in sales in 1983, observes:

> People in the industry know and respect each other but there's something in their personalities that makes them individualists. We don't form clubs—I don't belong to a country club or a Monday morning breakfast club. There's a business infrastructure but no real social structure in a place like Silicon Valley. I am as likely to socialize with a school teacher or anyone at Tandem as I am with any CEO in the Valley. Clubs, all that stuff, are old bureaucratic, anti–free spirit.

Although lacking in what some might call the social graces, this casual network of executives, commonly known around the Valley as "the support structure," constitutes a truly remarkable business innovation. In Silicon Valley, the aspiring entrepreneur has easy access to everything from venture capital and equipment leases to legal services and virtually any sort of technical advice. Due largely to the remarkable efficiency of this infrastructure, California continues to attract as much as 40 percent of the nation's total venture capital pool, despite high land and labor costs.[14] In the words of Silicon Valley public relations mogul Regis McKenna, these elements have created "a risk culture" in which talented technologists are virtually expected to leave the corporate ranks at least once during their careers.

Swept up by this "risk culture," young engineer Bob Metcalfe left his secure job at Xerox's Palo Alto research office in 1979 to follow the Valley's well-trodden path toward entrepreneurial success. Already renowned at 31 as the inventor of Ethernet, Xerox's pioneering new computer networking system, Metcalfe was widely considered the company's most promising young engineer. Yet despite his considerable corporate success, he was increasingly captivated by the examples of successful technological entrepreneurs all around him. Whatever doubts he might have had about leaving Xerox, moreover, were somewhat assuaged by the offer of several million dollars from local venture capitalists willing to back his new venture. Sitting in his cubicle at the Mountain View office of Three-Com, Metcalfe recalls:

> It's the lure of numbers. Xerox can make you comfortable but it can't make you rich. So you get out the Rolodex and you start calling. There's the infrastructure and the role models. The other engineers who have made it. If you want to start a company, you can get the backing. There's a script to follow.

One key problem facing Metcalfe, however, has been making the transition from inventor to entrepreneur. A self-described "white socks and plastic pen-in-the-holder nerd," he needed to learn about marketing, sales, finance, employee relations—things other people worried about at Xerox. "I was a tech tool," Metcalfe jokes. "Having this company allows me to be a backslapping salesman."

To direct the company and his own managerial training, he brought in a new president, former Hewlett-Packard executive William Krause, another corporate veteran anxious to achieve entrepreneurial success. Basing their strategy on the traditional Silicon Valley formula for small companies—specialization, technical excellence, and a focus on future market trends—Metcalfe and Krause consciously seek to duplicate the successful entry of other once small firms (such as Tandem) into markets previously dominated by corporate giants. "IBM must work to protect their installed base," Metcalfe says of his most formidable competitor. "They tend to move more slowly in the market than a smaller company."

Buoyed by early success, Metcalfe believes Three-Com is well on the way to emerging as a company on the scale of Intel. Daydreaming on a sunny afternoon, he thought out loud about *his* plans for Xerox. "I've told them I want to come back," the 34-year-old entrepreneur said with an impish grin, "when my company is ready to buy them out."

Although most prominent in the world of computer electronics, this new entrepreneurial risk culture also has begun to sweep over industries long thought impervious to small-scale operations. Four hundred miles south of Silicon Valley, in the sprawling suburban office parks of Orange County, entrepreneurs are breaking into the burgeoning biomedical industry, long dominated by such multibillion-dollar giants as Johnson and Johnson.

The key figure in Orange County's biomedical boom was a brilliant technologist, Lowell Edwards. A quintessential American tinkerer, Edwards turned a handsome profit into a fortune by developing a staggering array of innovations, including a debarker for the forest products industry, shower valves for the home, and parts for air force spy planes.

Edwards postponed a well-deserved retirement in 1960 after hearing about the problems faced in the development of artificial heart valves. Immediately entranced, he dropped everything and founded his own small laboratory out in Signal Hill, south of Los Angeles. Longtime aide Arnie Solberg recalls:

> He just thought there was more to life. He wanted to tackle more problems, more challenges. . . . Lowell took one look at the mechanical work that was being done in the field and knew they needed help. Doctors just didn't have the mechanical skill—but Lowell did.
>
> None of us knew much about the medical side when we joined Edwards Labs. There was no such thing as bioengineering.

From the beginning, Edwards made money by developing the heart valve and other innovations, then selling them to the large medical instrumentation and drug companies. Finally, in 1966, American Hospital Supply—then a $100 million firm—purchased the laboratory for roughly $2 million with an allowance for Edwards, by then in his seventies, to continue with his tinkering.

But if American Hospital Supply now owned Edwards Labs, they could not control the impact of the inventor's highly independent character on those coming to work with him. Edwards remained a rebel, refusing to wear ties or to kowtow to high-level corporate executives, preferring to work all night in his laboratory because, as one aide recalls, "His brain wouldn't shut down at night. If he was working on a problem he would sink his teeth in and couldn't let go."

By the time death caught up with Lowell Edwards in 1982, his highly independent spirit had suffused an entire generation of young executives brought up under his tutelage. Like the master, these innovators felt constrained in the corporate environment and many soon left it to start their own businesses. By the late 1970s, several former disciples of Edwards had built multimillion-dollar companies manufacturing, among other things, artificial lungs, heart valves from pigs, and surgical devices. One of these spin-off firms, Bentley Labs, was ultimately sold back to American Hospital Supply for over $200 million. When yet another of Edwards' protégés, a young biomedical engineer named Bruce Vorhauer, failed to interest company executives in his pet project—a new female contraceptive—the choice seemed clear:

> You spend a career seeing someone else do it. First Lowell, still at it in his seventies. Then all the other guys. Then you see your buddy start a company and sell it off for 80 million bucks. It sort of wakes you up and you say, Jesus, if those guys can do it, I can. I mean, this place is crawling with entrepreneurs who have done it.

Leaving Edwards in January 1976, Vorhauer, a Virginian with no real experience running a company, faced what seemed like impossible odds. Giant firms such as Johnson and Johnson, Warner-Lambert, and Parke-Davis already dominated the market; no one had successfully penetrated their dominion for decades. With only a small amount of capital from local Orange County gynecologists, Vorhauer doggedly pressed ahead with his plans.

In the process of starting up his firm, Vorhauer, like other entrepreneurs, found a new strength and identity, surprising even to himself. He felt suddenly liberated, able to dream the impossible and achieve it. Sitting in his Costa Mesa offices, Vorhauer recalls:

> In one month I got divorced, quit my job as the division vice-president, went on a diet, stopped wearing ties, started the company, moved to the beach. It was decompressing from years in big companies. I got it all out of the way.
>
> I learned real quick that the three most important things for an entrepreneur are tenacity, knowing you're right, and having a low bullshit level.

To assure "a low bullshit level," Vorhauer immediately opened up equity positions for everyone on the staff, from secretaries to highly skilled engineers. A strong sense of camaraderie arose among its twenty people as the company developed its product, an easy-to-use, two-day contraceptive sponge. By late 1981, things were well enough on the way to attract two prominent Chicago venture capitalists, Stan Golder and John Hines, President of Continental Illinois Ventures. A little over a year later, after a long tussle with the Federal Drug Administration, the new contraceptive won interim approval. As orders for his product came pouring in, Vorhauer, along with his staff and investors, prepared to reap their fortunes.

Vorhauer believes that the success of his and other biomedical firms demonstrates the increasing ability of small companies to enter markets previously dominated by big firms. By targeting their resources, taking risks, and harnessing the power of the intangible human factor, Vorhauer believes entrepreneurs can exploit their natural comparative advantage over their larger corporate competitors:

Lowell once told me that the big companies fail because they can only motivate through fear. A fearful man isn't a risk-taker. It's not the way to live or run a business. You can't be afraid of failure.

Here we work on a different principle. Everyone has a stake in making it. The secretaries are enthusiastic—they can make $50,000 on this deal—and the engineers are motivated like hell. We have the feeling of a team, a small team, and that's why we have succeeded where all those big medical labs have screwed up.

T. I. UNIVERSITY

Back in 1960, L. J. Sevin, a lanky engineer from the backwoods of Louisiana, rolled into Dallas to take a job at Texas Instruments, then a fast-growing and aggressive competitor to IBM and the other entrenched eastern giants of high technology. Rising through the ranks, by the late 1960s Sevin had emerged as a leading figure within the semiconductor division of the ascendant Texas firm, by then the world's top producer of integrated circuits.[15]

A man highly respected throughout the company, Sevin worked tirelessly to push the expansion of the company's promising new line of semiconductors. But behind the boardroom doors, Sevin found himself overruled by a top management already deeply committed to older technologies. Blocked by superior corporate gamesmen, the stubborn Cajun found himself in a dilemma. In those days Texas Instruments almost totally dominated Texas high tech, few engineers daring to leave its corporate embrace. But then a group of local Dallas high rollers approached Sevin with an offer of $250,000 to start a new company to be called Mostek. "I thought about it for about fifteen minutes," Sevin recalled as he drove his red Cadillac through the pristine streets of Dallas's posh northside. "That opportunity was one I couldn't turn down. If I had, I would have slit my throat by now."

Within the next decade, Sevin built Mostek into one of the nation's hottest semiconductor firms, garnering profits of over $9 million in 1978.[16] Spurred in part by Sevin's success, well over a dozen other TI executives have since left the giant firm to built their own companies. George Goode, a veteran TI engineer who broke away to found two highly successful companies in the past ten years, explains:

> TI trains its people very well. You learn to seek out business and solve problems. All of us who have been to TI know that TI is the world's greatest university where you get to conceive products, develop and market them. You learn to do what needs to be done. Anyone who works in a product center at TI already knows how to run a business. The problem is that after a while you figure out that you really don't need TI to help you. You ask yourself what are you going to do for the rest of your life—end up as an assistant vice-president of a division? TI told me that they need a $100 million market to make it worth their effort but I didn't need that much money. So I went off with a gleam in my eye.

Nine years after leaving TI, Goode sold his first company, Datotek, for some $3.5 million and almost immediately turned his attention to yet another start-up company. At George Goode and Associates, he and a highly skilled team of twenty-two technical personnel have developed microprocessors for a dozen products over the last two years, ranging from coin machines and heaters to computerized sugar mills. With annual sales of over $2 million, Goode's new company has even conducted training sessions for TI people, showing them how best to compete with the hard-charging Japanese.

The experience of former TI executives Goode and Sevin reflects the development in Texas of the same sort of risk culture so pervasive in California. Already the state ranks second only to California in the number of high-technology electronics firms and fast-growth companies on the *Inc.* 100 list.[17] With $140 million in venture capital pouring in, scores of technically-minded Texans are eschewing

their state's historic preference for the giant scale in favor of entrepreneurism. "If you have an iota of dream in you, in the end you
have to leave," Goode said, looking across the road at TI's gleaming
headquarters. "I'd bet in Dallas right now there are probably 1,000
engineers from LTV or Texas Instruments working on something in
their garages."

The idea of Texas as a hotbed for sophisticated manufacturing
would have seemed laughable only a few decades ago. From its days
as a Mexican colony well into the 1950s, Texas's economy was almost completely dependent upon its rich natural bounty of fertile
farmland and abundant supplies of oil and gas. Lured by these
riches, well-heeled interests from the industrialized North regarded
the state as little better than a resource colony, investing only in the
state's land and oil, not in the skill of its citizens.[18] To men such as
J. V. Farwell, one of a handful of Chicago capitalists owning the
three-million-acre XIT ranch in the panhandle, the state's paltry industrial base could be explained simply by "the slow brain and
muscle of the native Texas people."[19]

Only in the 1940s did Texas begin to shake its long reliance on
agriculture and oil. James Ling, a poor boy from across the Red
River in Oklahoma, and other ambitious young men migrated to
Dallas seeking their fortunes. After several years working in dead-
end restaurant jobs to make ends meet, Ling joined the Navy and
received training as an electronics technician. In 1947, scraping to-
gether $2,000 to purchase some war-surplus electrical equipment, he
started a small contracting firm. In the first year the hard-driving
Ling made $70,000, mostly installing light bulbs and other fixtures.
Soon he was working on large-scale projects, and by 1949 Ling
Electric was earning over $400,000 annually. After two decades of
wheeling and dealing on a scale titanic even by Texas standards,
Ling turned his little contracting firm into the basis of the $3 billion
LTV conglomerate, only to see it all but collapse in the early
1970s.[20]

Along with a handful of other industrialists including Ross Perot,
founder of EDS Corporation, Ling participated in the transforma-

tion of Texas from a colony of eastern interests into an international center. Between 1950 and 1960, the state's manufacturing employment jumped 34.6 percent, more than three times the national rate. And in the 1960s manufacturing growth jumped over 50 percent. By the 1970s the Texas high-tech and energy-oriented manufacturing complex was expanding nearly five times faster than the national average; by the end of the 1980s, this growth could allow Texas to overtake New York as the nation's second most populous state.[21]

As in California, Texas's relatively loose social structure helped ease the way for outsiders like Ling. Unfettered by the presence of a strong, entrenched elite, entrepreneurs from obscure backgrounds soon found that their wealth more than made up for their lack of lineage. As Stanley Brown, Ling's biographer, put it:

> An outsider can make it in Dallas society by having money, dressing neatly, giving away money. . . . The ruling group in Dallas is open to anyone who meets its qualifications. It is a democracy of money, an open society of businessmen.[22]

Within this "democracy of money," Texas Instruments stood out as Dallas's most enduring entrepreneurial success story. Founded by Clarence "Doc" Karcher, an Oklahoma farm boy with an abiding interest in applying science to oil exploration, the company started in 1930 as the Geophysical Services Company (GSI). Seeking ways to improve oil drilling and exploration efficiency, it drifted increasingly into electronics, eventually changing its name to Texas Instruments in 1951.[23]

This remarkable ability to move into new areas of endeavor assured Texas Instruments' emergence as a world leader in high technology. In 1947, when Western Electric offered licenses for its newly developed transistor to anyone willing to pay $25,000 in advance of royalties, the obscure Dallas firm sent its check in the next day. With only $27 million in annual sales—a pygmy compared to most of the other thirty-four firms with similar licenses—TI's small, technically oriented management recognized the virtually unlimited promise of the new circuitry far more keenly than its larger eastern competitors. Building upon this technological base, TI had transformed itself by the end of the 1960s from a medium-sized oil service firm into the world's leading producer of integrated circuits.[24]

But as the company grew, so did the dissension and dissatisfaction within its ranks. The new technologically oriented businessmen lured to "TI Hill" in North Dallas frequently grew attached to product ideas not within the company's highly structured corporate plan. In the early 1960s two of these frustrated engineers, Charles Skelton and Phil Ray, broke away to start International Data Systems and several years later moved down to San Antonio to start Datapoint, now a computer giant in its own right with sales of over $500 million in 1982.

Yet as in the Silicon Valley, the development of high-technology companies in Texas did not flow from one source; as new companies like Datapoint grew, they too had defectors repeating the cycle of entrepreneurial creation. "Some people are just start-up types," says one former Datapoint executive who is a key figure in two Texas start-ups. "Some of them roll, some of them don't, but you just pick yourself up and start again. We Texans don't give up easily once we know the game."

As he has for better than fifteen years, L. J. Sevin today remains the central figure in the development of the risk culture, Texas-style. After selling Mostek to United Technologies for $380 million in 1979, Sevin lasted a bare two years before returning to the entrepreneurial fray. "It's hard to be the prophet after being God," he jokes. "I just couldn't execute someone else's program."

After spending several months investigating possible new adventures with his partner, New York investment analyst Ben Rosen, they decided to enter the venture capital game. Starting his new career at 51, Sevin—along with Rosen—invested $25 million in sixteen companies, with interests ranging from communications technology and semiconductors to personal computers. Six of those companies are in Texas, where Sevin hopes to accelerate the development of the Lone Star State's high-technology risk culture.

The most spectacular of the Sevin-backed high-tech firms may well be Compaq, a new personal computer firm founded by three former TI executives. First brought together to help develop TI's new disk memory in 1979, three Houston-based engineers, Rod Canion, James Harris, and William Murto, left the firm only after a long and bitter fight over top management's failure to carry out their strategy for achieving "leadership technology" in the disk field. Taken off the disk project, team leader Canion felt compelled to reassess his career plans:

> If they hadn't screwed around, I'd still be at TI. I thought I was going to be a long-termer. I wasn't one of those dreamers who spends his life dreaming about starting a business. I didn't know the dream was even there. . . . We didn't know what our product would be but we knew we had to get out of the big company where everything was frustration, so we quit to go on our own and have fun.

"Fun" started around Christmas in 1981 as Canion, Murto, and Harris sat in their Houston living rooms day after day, trying to figure out a market niche for their new company. Training at "TI University" had made them think in terms of strategic development and marketing of product—now all they needed was an idea and some money. Finally, in late January, they hit upon the concept of building a powerful IBM-compatible portable business computer. Convinced they could find a market niche between the pioneering Osborne and Kaypro portable computers and IBM's personal machine, the engineers approached Sevin and Rosen. After some discussion, the venture capitalists shelled out $20,000 for offices on a handshake and Compaq was on its way.

With Sevin and Rosen behind them, the new managers were able to attract over $30 million in venture financing from across the country. Equally important, Compaq brought together some of computerdom's most skilled technical and management people, lured by the presence of such respected industry figures as Rosen and Sevin. "Everyone wants to go with L. J. because they know he's been there before," says Compaq's vice-president of manufacturing, John Walker, a 50-year-old veteran of Datapoint and several other high-tech ventures. "The man's a legend. L. J.'s the only man I would trust holding my wallet and my watch outside a brothel."

Backed by one of the largest initial venture capital fundings in high-tech's history, Compaq created over 300 new jobs within a year of its founding and expects to break into the $100 million annual sales range by 1984. But perhaps more important, the company's spectacular success could well encourage other Texans to take the entrepreneurial plunge. As L. J. Sevin sees it:

> The activity has been more concentrated in a few big places like TI. There haven't been as many start-ups but we're going to change all that. . . . You won't find a Silicon Valley here yet but we're going to fill this place with little companies. For entrepreneurs, this is a magical place.

MASSACHUSETTS: THE NONCONFORMIST'S ROAD

The economic "magic" now developing in Texas—as well as other Sunbelt states such as Florida, North Carolina, and Arizona—has largely bypassed the great industrial regions of the North and East. But Massachusetts, virtually alone in the old industrial belt, has experienced a miraculous entrepreneurial rebirth. After losing more than 250,000 manufacturing jobs (nearly one factory job in five) between 1968 and 1975, the state's increasingly high-tech economy produced a dramatic 17 percent increase in manufacturing employment between 1975 and 1980, a jump fifteen times greater than its mid-Atlantic neighbors.[25] With the recovery of its manufacturing base, Massachusetts now boasts one of the lowest jobless rates in the nation.

Sparking this remarkable performance has been a succession of young, dynamic entrepreneurial firms. In a pattern similar to that seen in both California and Texas, scores of new firms have been created by restless technologists fed up with life in large corporate and educational institutions. Successful outsiders such as Edson de-Castro, founder of Data General, and An Wang have inspired whole new generations of New England entrepreneurs; indeed, one 1980 survey found nearly 40 percent of the area's computer firms had been founded within the last five years.[26]

Once considered to be a most staid city, Boston is now a beacon for young, aggressive and stubbornly individualistic businesspeople. Comments James Howell, chief economist of the First National Bank of Boston:

> We attracted the best and the brightest from around the world—the sorts least prepared for institutional life. They gave a perfect deviant performance. They were the grist for the en-trepreneurs. . . . The risk-taking philosophy is deep in New England. It has long been tolerant of deviant behavior.

Nonconformism's roots in New England can be traced back to the Pilgrims. In the 1700s these tenacious dissenters from the cultural norms of their day, with their own odd ideas of religion and moral-ity, developed a powerful business culture in the new land; much to the chagrin of the clerics, many descendants of the first settlers proved more adept at business than religion. "A Bostonian," wrote one French observer at the time, "would seek his fortune in the bot-tom of hell."[27]

Hades, in fact, might have seemed more inviting, given the rocky soil and limited growing season of the Bay Colony. Yet the very par-simony of nature's endowment led New England to dominate the early industrial development of North America. Enterprising colo-nists turned to the vast forests and shipbuilding. By the time of the American Revolution nearly one-third of the ships flying the British flag were built in the colonies, mostly in New England.[28]

While some took these ships out on the sea to harvest the rich fishing grounds of the Georges' Banks, others sought quicker profits by preying upon the goods-laden vessels of unfriendly European powers. Some of New England's most prestigious families can trace their fortunes to such opportunistic adventurers. "They were pirates," Brahmin Godfrey Cabot would later say of his colonial forebears, "but now we're so refined we call them 'traders.' "[29]

These "traders," as well as more legitimate merchants, established Boston as the commercial hub of colonial America. Threatened by British mercantilist restrictions, John Hancock and other Boston merchants helped spark the 1775 rebellion against the Crown. When the rebellion drove scores of wealthy loyalist merchants from the city, historian Russell B. Adams observes, ambitious outsiders such as John Lowell arrived to exploit the huge commercial vacuum left behind.[30]

Even as the focus of trading activity shifted to the far more centrally located and superior seaport of New York, Lowell and other newcomers created the basis for the region's first great industrial boom. These early New England industrialists found new and efficient means to manufacture the shoes, textiles, and hats that would so long constitute the basis of the region's economy. In the 1840s, New England not only hummed with the prosperity of the mills, but also stood out as the nation's cultural leader.

As the nation pressed westward, however, into the age of iron and steel, the once adventurous Boston business establishment became increasingly entrenched and estranged from the great American economic drama. Speaking in the 1880s at the commencement of Boston University, the orator Edward Everett Hale noted:

The leaders in Massachusetts sixty, seventy, eighty years ago were the men who had done something. They had discovered the Columbia River or traded for furs with the Indians, or split ice off an iceberg in Labrador and sent it to Havana or Calcutta . . . the leaders of society now, whose most prominent business is to unlock a safe in a safe deposit vault and cut off the coupons from their bonds and carry them to be cashed . . . do not, to my mind, compare favorably.[31]

Under the tutelage of this elite, it is not surprising that New England's industrial base continued to decline for the better part of the next century. Instead of building up local industries, the region's money flowed out into distant, more profitable investments such as building a railroad in what Boston's Charles Francis Adams snidely called "that great, fat uninteresting West." Even as Bostonians played a major role in creating new companies, such as the Bell Telephone Company and United Fruit, power inevitably shifted to the more aggressive wheeler-dealers of Wall Street. Boston financiers, complained Frederic Stimson, had to "content themselves with the crumbs from J. P. Morgan's table."[32]

Yet as the elite grew ever weaker, new groups arose that were ultimately capable of reviving the moribund region. Native-born Yankees, better than three-fifths of Boston's population in 1860, were outnumbered three to one by outsiders at century's end.[33] Initially too poor and ill-educated to challenge the economic supremacy of the old Brahmin establishment, the progeny of these immigrants—Irish, Jewish, Greek, Italian, Portuguese, Oriental—would provide many of the entrepreneurs responsible for the region's eventual recovery.

Ultimately, it was the son of one of the most successful of the early immigrant entrepreneurs, Joseph Kennedy, who provided the spark for New England's new high-technology economy. Under his son John's administration, defense and NASA contracts flowed to the Boston area, enriching such emerging companies as Raytheon and Sylvania. From government-funded MIT-Lincoln Labs sprang Digital Equipment Corporation, perhaps the most important of the early entrepreneurial high-tech firms. By 1967 Massachusetts high tech employed 70,000 people and produced well over $1.5 billion in revenues.[34]

Unlike the owners of the shoe factories and mills, many of the key figures in this new entrepreneurial configuration came from outside the old Yankee establishment. From one remarkable family of Russian émigrés, the d'Abeloffs, emerged two of the regions most important innovative firms, Teradyne and Millipore, with 1981 sales of

$160 and $253 million respectively. A Greek immigrant, George Hatsopoulous, began his Thermo-Electron Corporation in a Belmont basement in 1956; by 1981 the company had grown into a major international force in the high-technology instrumentation and process control industry, with sales better than $210 million.[35]

Although some firms such as DEC and Thermo-Electron studiously avoided over-reliance on defense contracts, many Boston area firms suffered the same fate as their California cousins during the big post-Vietnam drop in military spending. Between 1970 and 1972, the Boston area lost 30,000 defense-related jobs; all along the Route 128 high-tech corridor engineers were reduced to driving cabs and slinging hash. "The process that got many of the Route 128 companies started," summed up Gerald Bush, then director of economic development for the city of Boston, "also predicted their failure."[36]

This debacle not only destroyed scores of small firms, but almost devastated such emerging titans as Raytheon which itself laid off 10,000 workers and engineers in the midst of the crisis. Large size—often a critical factor in the awarding of contracts through the Pentagon bureaucracy—did not facilitate the sort of flexibility needed to make the transition from defense to consumer products. Although Raytheon survived, reducing its reliance on military goods from 85 percent of sales in 1965 to 45 percent ten years later, the mantle of technological predominance now shifted, as it did in California, to smaller, more entrepreneurial firms.[37]

Helping this explosion of smaller, consumer-oriented firms was a small, risk-oriented group of venture capitalists. Inspired largely by the role model of General George Doriot, founder of the pioneering American Research and Development (ARD) Company, these new financiers challenged the traditionalist Boston banking and business establishment. Instead of investing their funds in insurance companies and other "prudent" investments, Doriot and other venture capitalists chose to back the technological ventures of aggressive young engineers. For the first time in over a century New England was no longer simply doling out dollars to other regions; it began to emerge as one of the most attractive locales in the nation for new venture investment. By 1981, with $239 million invested, the region was second only to California as recipient of venture funds. Sparked by this infusion, the region's high-technology firms enjoyed an over 34 percent sales growth and a 24 percent increase in new jobs between 1975 and 1980.[38]

By the late 1970s, the success of such ARD-funded firms as Digital Equipment Corporation, developer of the minicomputer, was further aided by a concerted state effort to support the development of high-technology firms. In exchange for tax concessions, the state's insurance companies, long the bastion of rock-ribbed conservatism, set up a $1 million fund to finance job-creating young firms, many of them in the electronics area. Other state programs, the Bay State Skills Center among them, helped supply entrepreneurs with skilled technical workers.[39]

Although the local government gradually assisted their growth, the key players in this industrial renaissance were entrepreneurs with few political and social connections within the traditional Yankee establishment. Sitting in his quaintly Victorian offices on Boston's windy Devonshire Street, Peter Brooke, a former executive at the First National Bank of Boston and now managing partner of TA Associates, founded in 1968 and one of the city's largest venture firms, recalls:

> The community generally looked askance at what we were doing. The establishment thought we were less than legitimate. I can't remember a pedigree type we've been involved with. . . . There are no entrepreneurs who are Yankees. They are still sitting around on their money. It's the environment of all the old men who put their money into Penn Central. None of the activity on Route 128 came from Yankees. That Yankee ingenuity stuff is a bunch of bullshit. If any Yankee tells you they did it, I'd read him the riot act.

Brooke, the son of a British immigrant, identifies ethnics, particularly the local Greek, Italian, and Jewish communities, as New

England's leading source of entrepreneurial talent. Like the Pilgrims and buccaneers of the colonial period, young ethnics growing up in New England felt the compulsion to establish a niche for themselves; rather than take to the seas, they explored the uncharted regions of the high-technology marketplace. The earlier successes of men like Chinese immigrant An Wang, whose electronics empire now employs over 13,000 people in the once economically devastated mill town of Lowell, helped establish outsiders as role models in the creation of a risk culture.[40]

Like other young ethnics growing up in working-class Boston in the 1950s, Art Pappas saw in the technical field a way out. Declining to follow the Greek immigrant stereotype by taking a job at the fishing docks or in a restaurant, he worked his way through night classes at Northeastern University. Graduating as an engineer in 1964, Pappas went to work for Epsco, a thriving Boston area high-tech firm with lucrative military and space contracts. Sensing that the government-funded bonanza was about to end, Pappas started designing his own products for industrial uses, including a 1967 power supply system adapted to high-technology manufacturing.

Undeterred by the deepening recession throughout New England, in 1969 Pappas, along with three partners, founded Datel, a high-tech firm making electric converters. Working as vice-president for finance, treasurer, and eventually manager of operations, Pappas played a key role in developing Datel into a moderately successful company. When acquired by Intersil in 1977, Datel sales stood near $20 million.

Suddenly a millionaire—with a 16 percent equity position in Datel before acquisition—the Greek engineer tried to fit into Intersil's developing corporate bureaucracy. Increasingly, he found himself frustrated by the slowness of decision-making at the $100-million firm. Driving through the New England countryside in his 1979 Volkswagen bug, the short, trim engineer remembers:

I did not like working for them—maybe I'm just not built for working for anyone else. It became impossible to operate as a free spirit. If we had a good idea, we used to be able to do it. I couldn't deal with writing reports and waiting six months. The people at Intersil were nice but I believe in a small market you have to move—and move fast. That's the only pace I like.

In 1980, frustrated by corporate life, Pappas approached Boston venture capitalist Bill Egan with designs for a new series of DC-DC power converters, capable of halving energy costs for computer users. It wasn't the most spectacular product in technological history, but Egan believed it served an expanding market. Banking largely on Pappas's track record at Datel, Egan helped raise $1 million to start the new firm, Power General.

Today, Art Pappas is doing what he likes to do—designing, manufacturing, and marketing a new product. Since opening for business in the heavily working-class Boston suburb of Canton, Power General's sales have climbed to over $4.5 million and are expected to double in 1984. Over 140 jobs have been created by the firm, most going to the area's poor but hard-working Portuguese immigrant community.

In those immigrant families Pappas sees a reflection of himself, of the little Greek boy coming off the boat in 1951 to the strange new world of America. Though his adopted land has been the scene of his success, he looks back to his outsider's roots to explain what drives him on:

Okay, I'm a millionaire and why start a second business? Maybe it's that I'm a Greek and always felt I had to prove myself. You know, Greeks are very individualistic—we're always fighting each other. Everyone has their own ideas. That's why we created so many philosophers. We are very ego-centered and we like to have things our way. I am the greatest and I want to prove it.

Very few Yankees I know are entrepreneurs. They don't have anything to prove, I guess. They're bankers and don't get into this sort of thing. Maybe, in a way, we're more like they used to be. Maybe we're the Yankees of today.

4

HEROES OF THE HEARTLAND

Even on the clear, crisp evenings at Christmastime, the shopping malls along the well-lit stretches of Kokomo's Markland Avenue seem nearly deserted, bleak and joyless. In the eerie quiet of the mall's long corridors, the unemployed sell cheap trinkets to those still lucky enough to hold a job.

With its steel mill, sprawling GM/Delco plant, and massive Chrysler factory, Kokomo, a town of 50,000 some fifty miles north of Indianapolis, once ranked among Indiana's most prosperous cities. During the halcyon days of the 1960s employment more than doubled while wages soared almost 250 percent. Today, however, as in many towns across the industrial heartland, the precipitous decline in the nation's basic industries has brought Kokomo's unemployment rate to a near Depression level of 20 percent and the local economy to the brink of disaster.[1]

Despite the gruesome realities, new leaders are emerging in Kokomo, determined to return the city to its once proud entrepreneurial roots. At the center of this renaissance is the attempt to revive Continental Steel, for over eighty years a bulwark of the local economy. Virtually bankrupt after fourteen years of control by the New York-based Penn-Dixie conglomerate, the old gray mill was taken over in 1981 by a group of locally based investors who faced the almost impossible task of turning around the battered and totally antiquated facility.

Led by its dynamic new president, Tom Sigler, Continental has slowly regained the entrepreneurial focus lost during the conglomerate era. While Penn-Dixie siphoned off some $35 million in company revenues to finance purchases of Florida real estate and other speculative ventures, the new management stands committed to the future of the steel industry and Kokomo. Under Sigler the firm's once dismal customer service has improved markedly, with on-time delivery rates jumping from 60 to 87 percent in less than two years. At the same time, a renewed emphasis on product quality and local markets has helped boost sales for the first time since the 1970s. A one-time millhand who still bears the scars from a furnace explosion thirty years ago, Sigler believes the progress at Continental underscores the increasingly central role that smaller scale entrepreneurial steel firms will play in the decades to come:

> We are making the future of American steel right here. What's needed is the entrepreneur who is committed to this business and willing to see it through the long haul. The people who are going to make the difference are the entrepreneurs and the workers, the guys getting their hands dirty.

In his attempt to revive Continental, Sigler is a throwback to the original business leaders who laid the red-brick foundations of the industrial town. Like a turn-of-the-century Silicon Valley, Kokomo once bustled with relentless entrepreneurs, men determined to turn the sleepy farming community toward the bold new age of machines and steel.

Among the most successful of these businessmen was a native Hoosier named Elwood Haynes. An inveterate tinkerer, Haynes created his first invention, a brass-making apparatus, before his sixteenth birthday and went on to develop a multitude of new products such as heat regulators, stainless steel, and cobalt-based alloys. In 1891, Haynes concocted the idea of building a gasoline-powered "horseless carriage." Three years later the nation's first commercial automobile, the Haynes Apperson, rumbled out of a Kokomo machine shop. Haynes's remarkable career reflected the inventive spirit of these earlier days. Other Kokomo businessmen produced such startling innovations as the pneumatic rubber tire, aluminum castings, the auto carburetor, and the all-transistor auto radio.[2]

In 1896, amid this heady entrepreneurial atmosphere, a group of local businessmen scraped together some $6,000 to found Continental Steel. Located down the road from Haynes's auto machine shop, Continental strove to serve the needs of the local market, starting with fences for farmers and expanding gradually to construction materials such as wire rods and nails. By 1903, the original $6,000 investment had matured into a $2-million company. Exceptionally well-run under local ownership, the company never laid off a worker—even in the Depression of the 1930s.[3] Howard Williams, whose father Art was among the firm's founders and later served as the company's marketing manager, explains:

> The community was everything to us back then. We were the biggest company in town. Our people were very good and we treated them right. We always kept up with the most recent changes. We felt we were the best darn steel company in the nation.

By the 1960s, however, Continental no longer dominated Kokomo. Major industrial giants such as GM, Chrysler, and the Cabot Corporation now provided Kokomo with most of its industrial jobs. A new, well-trained managerial elite imported from distant headquarters (as far away as Boston) brought with them a corporate ethic that rapidly supplanted the old spirit of entrepreneurial self-reliance. Over lunch at the local Elks Club, Dow Richardson, retired editor of the *Kokomo Tribune*, recalls:

> We used to be the envy of every town in Indiana because of all our auto plants. We never thought this would happen. We went

from being a locally owned place to being a big company place and never gave it a thought. We didn't even worry that the most important businessmen in town were suddenly guys just waiting to move up the ladder to Detroit.

Swept up by the culture of giant business, few of Kokomo's ambitious young men, except for those fleeing to other regions, dared even dream of establishing their own businesses. Indeed, when Purdue Professor Arnold Cooper visited the town's GM/Delco facility in the mid-1960s, the engineers there seemed totally uninterested in the exploits of other engineers in New England and California who were already building their own high-technology empires. Cooper later noted that the idea of leaving Delco to start their own firm seemed an almost inconceivable "step into the unknown."[4]

With the town's economic fate firmly in the hands of such risk-averse men and their distant bosses, few objected when the fast-rising Penn-Dixie bought up Continental in 1967. Under company head Jerome Castle, Penn-Dixie rudely cast aside Continental's veteran management team, replacing them with compliant, less experienced operatives. Product quality, almost an obsession under the original local owners, now was disregarded in a single-minded drive to generate the highest possible quarterly sales volume. In an equally serious move, Penn-Dixie also reversed Continental's tradition of giving priority to longtime local customers; during the 1973–74 steel shortage nearly 20 percent of the company's total output was diverted to a Castle crony, outraging many established customers. "We were told we could do nothing about it," remembers Rex Fager, a 29-year-old Continental veteran and now the company's marketing director. "Yet after the shortage, Castle's people totally deserted us."

As New York-based executives gained increasing control, Fager and other employees watched helplessly as Continental quickly deteriorated. The company was denied needed infusions of capital investments, and old equipment rusted and gradually broke down. So, too, did the once strong bonds between workers and management.

Bill Collins, the bullnecked president of the steelworkers' local, recalls: "You used to go up to a foreman and call him a son of a bitch and he'd call you a son of a bitch back. Then you'd finish work and have a beer with the guy. But with Penn-Dixie, everything sort of became like a war in the plant. They treated everyone like dirt."

In 1979, with federal fraud and conspiracy charges bearing down on him, Castle resigned from Penn-Dixie. But his legacy remained—a decimated company, steadily losing both its markets and well over $1 million a month. Faced with a deepening steel depression, beset by almost constant labor troubles, the company's future seemed bleak. Most Continental employees fully expected to find themselves standing on Kokomo's lengthening unemployment lines.

But the emergence of Sigler and his team of veteran steel executives has inspired new hope for the workers at Continental. Moves to improve quality and to correct distribution problems have impressed potential customers concerned about the company's long-term prospects. With other mills throughout the region closing down, reinvigorated Continental is now emerging as one of the most secure and reliable wire products producers within its large Midwest marketing region. "We're getting our old identity back," explains marketing man Fager. "We're a quality wire producer in the heart of the Midwest market, and we mean to service that market for a long time. Everyone's going to know we're back on the map."

Along with the new marketing strategy, Sigler has struggled to develop a new spirit of cooperation between the managers and workers at Continental. A wage- and benefit-slashing agreement with the steelworkers' union—in exchange for ownership of up to one-third of the company and a large share of future profits—played the crucial role in helping management win financing for an ambitious $38-million modernization scheme. With the new technological upgrading, Continental can boost its wire rod capacity by 30 percent while significantly reducing both per-ton costs and upgrading product quality.

Aided by these cost-cutting moves and its renewed marketing

focus, Continental executives expect to turn a healthy $10 million profit on less than $200 million sales by the mid-1980s, even without a general recovery in the steel industry. But perhaps more important than technology or marketing strategy, the human factor is back at work at the old mill, with workers and managers striving together to reverse a generation of corporate neglect. Drinking coffee in his cluttered, wood-paneled office early one winter evening, Sigler observed:

The future's going to be like that—either we all become entrepreneurs or we go down the tubes together. It's going to come down to the individual guy, in this office, on the line, his decision that this company just can't fail. Once people make up their mind about that, we can do almost anything.

RETURN OF THE NATIVES

Tom Sigler's struggle at Continental reflects an increasingly widespread effort by workers, managers, and risk-oriented financiers to save the nation's industrial heartland from utter devastation. New entrepreneurial forces in industries as diverse as steel, robotics, and machine shop services are bringing both new jobs and a much-needed venturesome spirit to the hard-pressed region.

Without the emergence of these industries and the service-oriented firms clustered around them, the heartland's prospects seem dim indeed. Although as much as one-fifth of the nation's GNP still comes from the steel belt's factories, mills, and shops, income and employment growth rates in the mid-Atlantic and mid-western states since the 1970s have grown at half the rate of the expanding Sunbelt. Many observers believe that under current conditions, this decline will accelerate during the next decade, leaving the area with fewer jobs in 1990 than it had at the onset of the 1970s.[5]

Stemming this tide will require a new direction for the Midwest, away from the remedies of corporate bail-outs, pork-barrel projects, and protectionism traditionally served up by Washington. Instead of trying to prop up the region's long dominant giant industries, the industrial belt must provide a more nourishing environment for the small manufacturing and service firms now providing virtually all the region's new jobs. Even as Michigan's auto-based economy began to crumble in the early 1970s, businesses with twenty or less employees generated enough new jobs to compensate for a 48-percent drop by all other size categories.[6]

Although still the predominant employer of production workers both regionally and nationwide, the giant manufacturers have been steadily losing jobs since the late 1960s. Between 1979 and 1981, large firms eliminated a half million manufacturing jobs, including tens of thousands in such key industries as automobiles and steel. At the same time, despite record bankruptcy rates, small businesses continued to offer new jobs.[7]

The job-producing prowess displayed by smaller firms has sparked new interest in locally based development throughout the nation's old industrial belt. Taking a cue from the successes of such Boston-based groups as Massachusetts Capital Resource Corporation, leaders in states across the heartland have set up new initiatives to encourage the formation of local entrepreneurial companies, including those in the older "sunset" industries.

For example, Pennsylvania's Millright Council (financed by both the state and private pension funds) is making special efforts to invest in or lend to "transition industries" seeking to apply new technologies to basic manufacturing. As Greg Robertson, executive director of the Council, explains:

I don't think we can write off our traditional industries at all. I think we have to make them more competitive in national and world markets. I think if we just focus on the entrepreneurial high-technology companies that will not be enough.

Although out of fashion with the prophets of a new "post-industrial" society, the new manufacturing jobs created by these small firms play a critical role not only for blue-collar workers but also for the rapidly expanding service sector now providing some 87 percent of all new jobs. Manufacturing is still responsible for about one-quarter of the GNP and one-fifth of the work force, and it provides the foundation for the growth of new service businesses. According to a University of Illinois study by economist A. James Heins, 100 new manufacturing jobs in a typical Illinois county engender the creation there of an additional 350 permanent positions and between 15 and 20 new retail or service establishments.[8]

"It's not a question of high tech or low tech, service or manufacturing," insists Elizabeth Hollander, executive director of Chicago's Metropolitan Housing and Planning Council. "We have to have both. Without those little manufacturing plants out in the unfashionable parts of town there wouldn't be the basis for everything else. They may not be the old guard, but if they leave the area, we're in deep trouble."

Chicago activists like Hollander are increasingly convinced that their city's future, long tied to giant industry, lies in the cultivation of its local entrepreneurial sector. During the 1970s Chicago suffered a net loss of more than 18,000 small firms—over 15 percent of the area's total—while states such as California, Texas, Florida, and Massachusetts were enjoying a tremendous upsurge in new firm creation.[9] Some Chicago leaders believe that this massive exodus was accelerated by the reluctance of top corporate executives and banks to involve themselves in the urban community beyond their lakeside high-rise fortresses. In his office on Michigan Avenue, Dean Douglas Lamont of the Roosevelt University School of Business reflects:

We need to develop a new entrepreneurial community. The people who settled this town came here to be merchants, traders, small business owners, industrialists. They were dreamers. Now most of the businesses in town are owned by outsiders, New Yorkers, foreigners.

This is the tragedy of Chicago and the Midwest today. There are very few people willing to take risks, to make the decisions we need to make. We have to fall back on ourselves, on our locally owned businesses, on the guys who can't just pick up and leave because no one else is listening.

THE LORDS OF CREATION

The spirit of self-reliance expressed by Lamont and Continental's Tom Sigler recalls the early days of America's heartland. The pioneers settling the region were, for the most part, rough and ill-educated, rejected by the more settled, caste-ridden society of coastal America. Swelling their numbers were millions of ambitious immigrants from Germany, Norway, and Sweden, anxious to break the shackles of European society and fulfill their long thwarted ambitions.

These settlers struggled doggedly against disease, lawlessness, and blight in order to build their new homes. In the process, they developed an innovative, risk-taking spirit that characterized the Midwest's early economic development. As historian Frederick Jackson Turner, a longtime resident of Wisconsin, wrote:

> The men and women who made the Midwest were idealists and they had the power of will to make their dreams come true. Here also were the pioneer's traits—individual activity, inventiveness, and competition for the prizes of the rich province that awaited. . . .
> He [the pioneer] honored the man whose eye was quickest and whose grasp was strongest in this contest. It was every man for himself.[10]

Amid this wide-open, often ruthless struggle for predominance cities such as Cincinnati and St. Louis rose within one generation from tiny frontier outposts to the status of major centers, fit rivals for the great seaport towns of the Atlantic. With unparalleled vigor, the region became the center for many of the great industries of the day—from railroads and beef to steel and, ultimately, autos—and by the early years of the 20th century possessed a population and industrial might greater than the older, eastern states. Determined to maintain their industrial and agricultural prowess, local governments across the heartland developed a remarkable system of public universities producing twice the number of eastern college graduates. Indeed, the rich wheat fields, the new schools, and the factories of the rapidly growing midsection prompted even so venerable a New Yorker as Theodore Roosevelt to consider the area "destined to be the greatest, the richest, and most prosperous" in the nation.[11]

Nowhere did the heartland's imperial destiny seem more manifest than in Chicago. A tiny settlement of some 350 French traders, Indians, and half-breeds (*métis*) in 1835, Chicago exploded to a population of over 300,000 by 1870. Men such as Marshall Field, Aaron Montgomery Ward, and Richard Warren Sears all came to Chicago seeking a better future. These merchants built their empires by introducing new ideas—money-back guarantees and mail order catalogues among them. Others, such as Cyrus Hall McCormick, a Virginia farm boy, developed the implements needed by the region's huge agricultural sector. McCormick's reaper, first developed in 1834 and mass-produced at a Chicago factory by 1847, transformed the nation's farming economy irrevocably. A business innovator as well as inventor, McCormick pioneered such tactics as credit selling and mass advertising, laying the foundation of the International Harvester empire.[12]

Virtually every midwestern city was built on the vision of such entrepreneurs. In Pittsburgh, for instance, the key player was Andrew Carnegie who, starting without significant education or resources, built a sprawling empire in 19th-century "sunrise" industries: steel, railroads, and oil.

The most successful ventures were frequently those flying in the face of convention, risking all on a new marketing concept or product idea. Few of the nation's pampered elite would have shared the obsession of John F. Queeny, a cigar-chomping Irishman from Chicago with only six years of education, about the potential of an obscure, newly discovered artificial sweetener called saccharin. Since the cost of saccharin was over seventy times that of sugar, most top business leaders saw little future in the new substance in 1901. Local drug firms flatly rejected Queeny's idea; needing $5,000 to start his own factory, he could not convince local bankers to lend him the money. Finally, in 1901, the Irishman scraped together his own funds plus a loan of $3,500 from a Chicago soft-drink firm and launched his new company, calling it Monsanto after his wife's maiden name. Trusting his own "seat of the pants" vision that mass production could ultimately drive down the cost of saccharin, Queeny established a viable alternative to natural sweeteners and in the process laid the foundation for one of the world's leading drug companies. As his son Edgar would later recall:

My father did it all somewhat as a challenge, somewhat on an impulse, but largely because he was sure it could be done. Market research? If he had taken time to accumulate the kind of data that is commonplace today, he probably would never have started the company. If all the information he needed on saccharin could have been fed into a computer in 1901, the computer would have blown a fuse.[13]

THE PACIFICATION OF THE MIDWEST

Yet as Queeny, Carnegie, and other entrepreneurs were building their empires, they also sowed the seeds of the giantism that later hastened the heartland's decline As industries such as steel expanded, a Schumpeterian "wave of creative destruction" obliterated thousands of small and medium-sized firms. From the 1880s to 1904 mergers absorbed over 5,200 independently owned industrial plants, costing a remarkable $7 billion—roughly 40 percent of the nation's manufacturing capital.[14]

The legacy of that first great merger wave still permeates the region; with nearly thirty-one of the nation's largest industrial corporations, the heartland remains, outside of the New York area, the nation's most giant-dominated region.[15] Forged by entrepreneurs, the new industrial combinations took the mantle of power from the independent industrialist and placed it squarely on the shoulders of the financier and professional manager. Even Carnegie, a man deeply distrustful of "finance capitalism," felt himself compelled in 1901 to sell his steel holdings to the Morgan interests for over $200 million.[16]

Carnegie's legacy, the new $1-billion U.S. Steel Corporation, became but the first of a new chain of impersonal mega-empires soon to dominate the heartland. Perhaps the most important of these was the automobile industry which, after a brief period of intense competition, soon became tightly controlled by three giant firms.

As Schumpeter and others have pointed out, the increasing economies of scale in such industries as steel and automobiles resulted in the demise of the entrepreneurial function. With millions needed to build new plants or acquire competitors, industrialists increasingly fell under the sway of Wall Street and other large financial interests.[17] At General Motors, for instance, founder W. C. Durant's expansion plans required a close alliance with both major banks and the DuPont family. When revenues fell during the 1919 recession, the bankers moved to take control, forcing Durant to surrender to a new team headed by Pierre DuPont and his staff of expertly trained managers, led by the legendary Arthur Sloan.[18]

By the 1930s the era of the great automotive entrepreneurs like Durant and Henry Ford was coming to a close. A new generation, rising up through the corporate bureaucracy, rapidly took their place.[19]

With the ascendancy of men like Sloan, married to the gospel of "management by methods and objective facts,"[20] the once vibrant entrepreneurial culture of the heartland's automobile industry began to dissipate. Under their guidance, the region became one of the most concentrated of the nation's economic sectors. By the early 1960s the four largest firms controlled over 80 percent of the automobile and 50 percent of the steel industry assets, the twin pillars of the heartland economy.[21]

In scores of factory towns such as Kokomo, this new industrial order meant that workers became vassals within a huge system of industrial feudalism. Although many great corporations took their local obligations seriously, few could feel the same depth of commitment to the community as local small or medium-size company proprietors. Studies in Wisconsin, Nebraska, Maine, and Iowa have found that outsider-owned firms are far less likely to create new jobs or preserve old ones than locally based businesses.[22] As T. K. Quinn, a former vice-president at General Electric, has pointed out:

> The manager is not part of the community in which he lives because his interest and attention is directed toward officials in New York or elsewhere. He is dependent on them for his job, his income, and his progress. He cannot have the same interest in the people employed at the plant. He operates according to rules made by others—handed down to him.[23]

The merger wave of the 1960s greatly accelerated the heartland's dependence on giant corporations, many based in distant locales. Between 1955 and 1968, 210 separate Illinois-based firms with over $2.6 billion in assets fell under outside control. Other major losers from the merger wave included New Jersey, Michigan, Nebraska, Pennsylvania, and Indiana.[24]

All too often the new masters of industrial concerns such as Penn-Dixie at Continental Steel lacked even a minimal commitment to the communities and industries whose fates they now controlled. Veteran manufacturing and marketing-oriented managers frequently found themselves under the thumb of financial experts with little experience or interest in the acquired firm's industry. At such tightly centralized conglomerates as ITT, with as many as 265 subsidiary corporations,[25] detachment from particular product lines assumed the character of a business virtue. As one top ITT official put it:

> If you are responsible for a single product such as cars or hotels, you tend to become too involved with it, too attached to

it. But here you can't fall in love with a thousand different products. So it doesn't bother you in the least to get rid of one that is no longer paying its way.[26]

When the climate for basic manufacturing worsened in the 1970s and early 1980s, such men had ample opportunity to display their indifference. Faced with mounting competition from abroad, many large companies in fields from autos and steel to consumer electronics chose to shift their manufacturing facilities outside the heartland, rudely casting many of their longtime workers into the abyss of unemployment.

Midwestern cities and towns such as Kokomo, for decades the prime beneficiaries of giantism, fell victim to corporate decision-makers in Detroit or New York office suites. During the 1970s alone the industrial belt lost over two million manufacturing jobs. In most cases, the firms deserting the region did not concern themselves overly with the impact on the towns left behind—only one of the fifty members of the Conference Board, a New York-based association of giant businesses, had, as late as 1983, developed any policy for dealing with the social consequences of plant closings.[27]

Although other states also suffered from plant closings, the impact of these closures in the Midwest was not offset by an explosion in new emerging industries. Unlike California and Massachusetts, states such as Illinois did not benefit greatly from the rise of the computer and other high-technology products. During the late 1970s high-tech jobs in Illinois increased at less than a third the rate of equally chilly Massachusetts and Minnesota.[28]

The heartland's failure to take full advantage of the high-technology explosion has little to do with its basic industrial infrastructure. Illinois and Indiana have some of the finest engineering schools in the nation. Chicago boasts superb research facilities, among them Argonne National Laboratories and a large venture capital community capable of wooing the wayward scientist.[29] But Chicago, along with much of the Midwest, has lacked the critical, irreplaceable element—a community of entrepreneurs willing to take risks. Ed Marlin, assistant director of economic development for the state, explains:

We should have been the ones to get these industries. We had Zenith, Admiral, and all those electronics companies of the fifties. But everything sort of migrated out of here. . . . You never got the spin-off here like you had on Route 128 or in Palo Alto. The path isn't real well known. Maybe the problem was we had it too good for too long. The success of our big companies made us too complacent. The entrepreneurial spirit wasn't there when we needed it.

THE NEW MEN OF STEEL

Among the ruins of the region's shattered economy, however, there are signs of a modest entrepreneurial rebirth. Burgeoning high-technology and service firms—such as Pittsburgh's Three Rivers Computers and Omaha's Godfather's Pizza—have begun to bring new life to the regional economy. Other entrepreneurs have found profitable niches in the low-tech manufacturing sector. Even in steel, the most basic of basic industries, a new generation of leaders is emerging, capable of salvaging profitable businesses that are the castoffs of the major firms.

Like many of the region's new men of steel, Cliff Borland seems an unlikely entrepreneur. A native of Pittsburgh, the soft-spoken, rotund executive followed his father and older brother into the supposedly secure world of big steel. Working his way up through the ranks at Interlake, a billion-dollar Chicago-based conglomerate, Borland eventually won the position of manager of the firm's Newport, Kentucky steelworks. Although constantly at odds with his bosses over the best utilization of the Newport facility, Borland looked forward to a long, comfortable career within the middle ranks of the company's managerial aristocracy.

But in 1980 Borland's pleasant little scenario fell apart. Dissatisfied with the mill's performance and eager to diversify away from steel, Interlake's top management decided to resolve their problems and shut down the Newport facility. Suddenly, Borland found himself cut off, without a job or prospects. Desperate, he searched for some way to keep the old mill alive. In his austere office in a seamy industrial district across the river from Cincinnati, the 45-year-old Borland recalls:

> It was either become an entrepreneur or go out on the steel job market—which isn't exactly great for a steel guy these days. I didn't even think about the possibility of starting something until the axe fell. I didn't know about entrepreneurs until I became one.

By putting up virtually all their life savings and raising money from several risk-taking financiers, Borland and three other top managers bought the mill for some $23.5 million and reopened it eight months after Interlake had shut it down. The newly constituted Newport Steel Corporation came to life in the midst of the worst steel recession since the thirties. Although Borland and his management team had never had total responsibility for a company before, they had faith in the value of their on-the-line experience. "We believed we could make a go of it where Interlake couldn't," the steel executive said. "There's a formula that allows you to make money if you're efficient and know your markets, even in bad times."

For Newport, the formula turned out to be simply implementing the suggestions Borland had been making for years to his superiors at Interlake with little success. Dropping the highly unprofitable rolling mill, he focused all efforts on Newport's more lucrative tubular products line. In addition, he also persuaded the steelworkers' local that his "lean and mean" approach to managing was the only way to save the mill, winning their tacit acceptance of a drastic reduction in salaried and hourly personnel from a pre-shutdown high of 1,100 to under 530. Through these savings and other efficiency moves, Newport Steel realized a substantial profit in its first full year of operation.

Today Cliff Borland seems comfortable in his new role. Launching a new $50 million modernization drive, he now seeks to boost Newport's pipe-making capacity from 180,000 to well over a half million tons. Although Newport's expansion plans mean a direct struggle against such giants as U.S. Steel, Borland feels convinced his smaller firm can outperform the industry leader. "I'm optimistic this industry will come back. Maybe not everyone in it—but the strong and the efficient will survive. Maybe that's what recessions are for, weeding out the weak and the lame. What's going to shock people is when they find out who the weak and lame really are."

Bolstering the confidence of Borland and other new steel entrepreneurs has been the rapid dissolution of the nation's long dominant steel giants. Since 1978, five major steel companies have gone bankrupt, and several other large firms—including the multibillion-dollar leviathans of Bethlehem, National, Republic, and Wheeling-Pittsburgh—could face bankruptcy within this decade, according to a recent report by the highly respected Oppenheimer and Company investment banking firm. Even without such a disaster, steel experts predict that as many as fifteen million additional tons of capacity could be taken out of production by 1985.[30]

In their hasty retreat from the industrial battlefield, the major steel firms, many veteran steel observers believe, have opened wide markets for the smaller, more efficient firms. "Their failures have been so great that they've created tremendous opportunities for entrepreneurs," observes Frank Cassel, former vice-president of Inland Steel. "Whenever there's a buck to be made, you'll find that the entrepreneurs come out of the closet."

While the majors have continued to blame steel's problems on foreign competition and looked toward Washington for assistance, the new heartland steel entrepreneurs model their strategy on the "mini-mills" that have grown so spectacularly in the nation's Sunbelt over the past two decades. Focused on local market needs, small steel firms such as North Carolina-based NuCor and Florida Steel have turned the Southeast, in the words of steel consultant Richard Dielly, into "a gestation area, a nursery . . . [for] the art of conceiving, building, and operating" mini-mills. Due largely to the presence of NuCor and six other major mini-mills, over the last two decades the Southeast has bucked the general national decline in steelmaking, increasing its share of the nation's steel market by some 50 percent while boosting production nearly 70 percent. Even more remarkable, many of these companies have maintained levels of profitability two to three times those of the giant steel firms.[31]

In marked contrast to the large, integrated producers, the southeastern-based mini-mills focus almost exclusively on one or two narrow product areas. And unlike the MBA-dominated giants, they tend to be run by metallurgists and other steel professionals. While U.S. Steel's David Roderick was demanding protection from foreign imports and spending over $6 billion to buy Marathon Oil, mini-mill executives such as NuCor's Ken Iverson were investing in new scrap-fed electric furnaces and other equipment needed to take on foreign challengers. Showing their commitment to steel in the face of soft demand, mini-mills have boosted their capacity over the past decade by eleven million tons while the integrated producers surrendered some twenty-two million tons of production. "It is fairly obvious where our segment of the industry is going," Florida Steel chairman Ed Flom states flatly. "We will grow."[32]

Equally important, like Silicon Valley companies such as Tandem Computers and Hewlett-Packard, many mini-mills are acutely aware of the importance of the human factor. Chaparral Steel in Texas and NuCor place special emphasis on employee bonuses; at NuCor incentive pay can augment salaries by as much as 51 percent.[33] At the same time that NuCor has expanded into the nation's tenth largest steel company, President Ken Iverson has worked assiduously to avoid creating yet another unwieldy steel bureaucracy. Instead of erecting a high-rise citadel for privileged managers, Iverson houses his key fifteen-member staff in a modest Charlotte office building.

This innovative management helped make NuCor one of the very few steel firms in the nation to make a profit during the horrendous 1982–83 slump. Even more remarkable, operating from its new Plymouth, Utah mill, NuCor has begun to cut Japan's share of the

California steel rod and bar market from 50 to 10 percent.[34] This triumph suggests that entrepreneurial drive and marketing might offer a better way to meet the foreign steel challenge than the protectionism long demanded by the giant firms. Comments one NuCor disciple, Continental's Tom Sigler:

> Right now Ken Iverson is The Force in steel. He's shown that the small companies with the new technology are paving the way—not the Inlands or the U.S. Steels. He's shown that despite all you hear, there's still a future in steel.

The key to survival in steel's future, Sigler and other new entrepreneurs know, will be the ability to take market niches away from both domestic giants and foreign competitors. With its large upholstery, appliance, and wire converter industries, the twelve-state heartland region around Kokomo is the nation's predominant consumer of the wire products that comprise some 85 percent of Continental's output. Closings by five major midwestern steel firms have taken 900,000 tons of wire capacity off the market, leaving foreign and southeastern United States producers as the company's chief competitors. By exploiting its location close to the major consumers of wire products, Continental enjoys a 10-percent transportation cost advantage over suppliers from outside the heartland.

The new men of steel also hope to take advantage of other changes in the marketplace. With the decline of the domestic car industry and the shift to smaller, lighter vehicles, the demand for sheet steel—long the major product of the giants' massive integrated mills—has slackened noticeably. But other product lines, particularly high-carbon alloys and specialty steel, could continue to increase markedly and provide potential growth markets, according to a federal Office of Technology Assessment Study.[35]

To industry veterans such as Calumet Steel's Jim Mertz, the rapid pace of change in the steel market seems likely to alter the basic structure of the industry. Long dominated by economies of scale, Mertz believes that the advantage in the future will belong to small-scale, efficient, and highly flexible mills. The stocky accountant, who led a management buyout of Borg-Warner's Chicago Heights plant back in 1975, observes:

> To a large extent we are watching a giant industry transforming itself into a Third Wave, cottage-style industry. Maybe demand will come back . . . but the problem will be surviving until that happens. It's like playing poker-in-reverse, to force the others out you're going to have to cut price. Until the giants leave the table, nothing is accomplished. Until then, we're just playing a game of very high stakes poker.

Despite obvious risks, the potential rewards of winning Mertz's "game of very high stakes poker" are already luring new entrepreneurs into the heartland's steel industry. Like 27-year-old Jim Lyons, some believe the rapid rate of plant closures could turn the persistent steel glut of the early 1980s into a severe shortage by the end of the decade. Indeed, one major federal study predicts a shortfall so severe that if no new capacity is added, foreigners could double their steel exports by the end of this decade.[36]

To meet this projected shortage, Lyons plans to construct a new $55-million, 150,000-ton mill in rural Indiana County, some thirty miles from the steel industry center at Pittsburgh. Massive cutbacks by giant firms in the area, slicing greater Pittsburgh's share of the national steel market in half and laying off some 45,000 workers over the past decade, have created a sizable niche for a new mill, Lyons believes. He explained: "All the big guys are leaving. There's all that scrap to burn and all those people hungry for a job. There's room for a mill here, at least a small one."

Despite his youth, Lyons considers himself a steel industry veteran with a proven record of success. A native of Ebensburg, a small village located on the plateau east of Pittsburgh, Lyons grew up among steelworkers and miners. At 19, he quit school to take over his family's fledgling cable and furnace repair business, turning it into a highly profitable service enterprise within five years. Today

Lyons's mini-mill proposal has made him somewhat of a folk hero in his native area, which is far more accustomed to seeing established firms die or move away.

Although some older hands consider Lyons's quest for a new mill utterly quixotic, he has won the support and assistance of such major engineering firms as Danielli, Italy's leading builder of mini-mills. Lyons may yet be far from his dream of becoming "the Steve Jobs of steel," but his determination proves the resiliency of entrepreneurism even in the hardest hit industries of the heartland:

> I believe in this industry, in its people and traditions. They're hard-drinking, plain-talking, and hard-working. They're not down, just beaten down. They want to come back. What's needed is the spark to get things going again. I know everybody is supposed to have his head in a computer these days, that's all anyone ever talks about. So you ask—what the hell is a young guy doing in steel? I'll tell you why. Because no one else is there.

THE NICHE-MAKERS

When the massive steel mills began to close, death came to the southside of Pittsburgh. Along the bluffs overlooking the Monogahela River, the gray hulks of deserted factories rust in the drizzle of early winter. Where furnaces once roared and foundries belched, weeds now grow amid the desolate remains of bankrupt companies.

On his street Harold Hall runs virtually the only business still in operation. A short, gray-haired man, Hall has survived the industrial holocaust through a remarkable knack for finding niches others have ignored. Instead of relying on the leavings from steel and other major manufacturing firms, in recent years Hall has feverishly expanded into diverse new areas; to his old machine shop business, he added metal fabrication, contract manufacturing, and a host of other services. Hurrying through his old rundown two-story headquarters, Hall stopped long enough to explain:

Several years ago we sensed the crisis and worked like hell to beat it. So we got away from our dependence on steel work, we looked for other projects. We had no choice if we wanted to survive. Our strategy has been to fill voids wherever they come up. The key is being able to shift our whole effort almost overnight. We have to anticipate needs before they occur. If we didn't, I'd be sweeping the floors.

A critical factor in Hall's recent profitability has been his sharp focus on the few opportunities for steel-related work in Pittsburgh—the new city subway and repair of the city's elaborate but worn-down bridge system. By concentrating on these and other potential growth areas, Hall has doubled his business since 1981 to over $5 million annually and boosted his work force to over 100 employees. Not content with present success, the 61-year-old entrepreneur is gearing up to enter the rapidly developing robotics design and maintenance field.

Once virtually ignored by the city's ambitious young men, surviving small businesses like Hall's have achieved a luster once reserved for the denizens of the steel and glass towers downtown. With Pittsburgh's big steel economy in a shambles, small firms have become the most attractive alternative for those interested in learning how to run a successful business. "Half the people working here now are under thirty-five," Hall says proudly. "Ten years ago these young people wouldn't have thought we were worth talking to. Now *we* get the hotshots from Carnegie-Mellon."

This new interest in small business reverses a nearly century-long Pittsburgh obsession with giantism. For generations the Mellons and families like them have all but controlled Pittsburgh society. Major corporations, four of the nation's fifty largest, had their headquarters in the city, as many as any city outside New York. This combined weight of wealthy, old-line families and giant corporations worked to stifle the city's small business development. Comments Dwight Bauman, professor of engineering design and director of the Center for Entrepreneurial Development at Carnegie-Mellon University:

This city is a very institutionalized place. Pittsburgh is a very clubby town—socially and organizationally. It's all third generation of industry. They don't even remember the spirit of the founders. . . . Most of them don't give a damn about the region because old man Mellon isn't around to make them. That's why independent business has to show the way and provide the alternatives.

Bauman, who has helped finance several new entrepreneurial firms through the center, maintains that the key to the future of the industrial belt lies in the marriage of high technology to the region's small manufacturing companies. Fortunately, the cost of such advances as computer-controlled design and manufacturing systems (CADCAM) is rapidly decreasing. Small computers are already operating in thousands of industrial plants. San Diego-based Action Instruments recently released an "industrial apple" costing under $5,000, capable of running complex factory operations. Even full-scale computerized manufacturing systems, now widely priced at $150,000 and up, are sliding down the cost curve.[37] Already Cadlink, an Illinois-based CADCAM firm, offers full systems for as little as $25,000, well within the reach of many small-scale metal foundries.

At Cadlink, this marriage of high technology with traditional heartland small manufacturing has proven a profitable one indeed. Located in the heart of Chicago's "Sheet Metal Valley"—the nation's largest foundry and machining center[38]—Cadlink markets extensively to foundries and machine shops across the nation, the vast majority of whom are small businesses with under 100 employees. Taking advantage of this market, Cadlink has weathered recessionary conditions and boosted sales of its computerized manufacturing systems from $1.5 million to over $10 million in sales since 1981. Cadlink president John West, a former factory worker himself, states flatly:

I have a personal thing about saving smokestack America, but it won't be with the large companies. They have their heads in the sand. When you think of manufacturing, you think of these huge plants, but now, with this technology the small guys—the job shops—might be a hell of a lot more efficient. The pendulum swings and it's swinging to the smaller shops.

Although excited by the possibilities of this new technology, veterans of Sheet Metal Valley believe the combination of old-fashioned ingenuity and aggressive marketing will continue to be the greatest determinants of success for small manufacturing firms. Located in a deteriorating neighborhood on Chicago's near northside, Sandy Carrigan's United Wirecraft, for example, hardly seems like a hotbed of industrial innovation. Yet inside the creaky old plant, United Wirecraft hums with the energy of a high-tech startup.

Founded in the early 1960s by Sandy's father, a former golf caddy, United has enjoyed steady 10 to 15 percent growth for the last fifteen years. Originally specializing in golf carts, the company now makes most of its money doing specialized jobs using wire and other materials. "This is a tough business. You have to move fast to keep up with the market," Carrigan maintains. "We rarely do the same job twice. Something that works for Levis now may not work next year."

In building a profitable $4-million business such as United Wirecraft, simple ingenuity sometimes proves more useful than the most advanced technology. Unable to find a welder to fit his needs, Carrigan characteristically went out and designed his own. With the help of his multiethnic work force (made up largely of blacks, Chicanos, and Poles), he built a machine perfectly suited to the company's needs for $35,000, markedly less than a store-bought model. Carrigan's contraption looks a little like a cross between a giant mousetrap and a piece of conceptual art, but it works.

With the new machine, one worker could do the work of five, allowing for considerable savings. But even in the face of tough economic conditions, Carrigan could not bring himself to lay off any of his longtime employees. "I just decided we wouldn't participate in the recession," he recalls cheerfully amid the clanging of the shop. "We know every one of these people and their kids personally. The people have a spirit like a family and I wasn't about to break that up."

To keep the company growing, Carrigan looked for new applications and new markets for an old business. After searching for months, he discovered a huge opportunity—building software display racks for a San Francisco high-tech firm. Standing, arms folded by his homemade welder, Carrigan observes:

That happens to us every day. But it's nothing for us. We may be in an old industry, but we still can solve your problems for you. They told us there was no solution to the software display problem. So I hopped on the plane and went to San Francisco. They didn't know what to do but I knew there was a solution. It took a while but we got the design. They want it tomorrow—and they'll get it.

5

BANKING ON PEOPLE

For nearly seventy years, even after its founder's death in 1965, Helena Rubinstein was among the most profitable and widely respected skin care firms in the country. Lured by this record of success, the giant Colgate toiletries company purchased Rubinstein in 1973 for some $143 million. In the words of one Colgate executive at the firm's Park Avenue headquarters, it seemed like "a perfect fit," adding the glamour of Rubinstein's products to the giant firm's more mundane line of toothpaste and soap.

But the acquisition of Rubinstein turned out to be a total disaster. Long profitable under independent management, by 1978 Rubinstein was losing over $30 million annually, its once strong high-fashion identity obscured within the vast constellation of Colgate. The same Wall Street analysts who had widely praised the initial takeover were now pressuring Colgate to divest itself of the dying company. Top management at the conglomerate were more than willing. The only problem was that no one seemed willing to take the firm off their hands. Bill Weiss, now Rubinstein's chairman, recalls:

What Colgate tried to do was to take a quality skin care company and go for the volume. They took the company from a high platform identity and threw it down into the street. They brought in new managers who didn't know the business so when it failed they stripped it. It was money management.

But Weiss, a New York attorney and veteran commercial finance executive, saw the elements of a great opportunity in Colgate's predicament. Like other practitioners of the art of entrepreneurial finance, Weiss looked beyond the numbers and concentrated on the human factors. In Rubinstein's dedicated staff, its well-established trademark, and traditional market focus, he saw the chance to rebuild the once proud firm. "I knew it was the deal I had waited twenty years for," the large, balding Weiss remembers in his cluttered Manhattan office. "Colgate kept saying they'd turn it around but that was bullshit. They didn't really have the motivation—but we had to live or die. We wanted to bring the grand old lady back."

In April 1980 Colgate accepted Weiss's offer of $20 million—only $5 million in cash—to take over the firm. Weiss became Rubinstein's new chairman and, together with his investors and veteran entrepreneur Harry Polly, moved quickly to resuscitate the company. Seeking to exploit the firm's traditional strengths in marketing and product development, he suspended the costly manufacturing operation, cutting the work force from 750 to 200. Executives with extensive cosmetics experience, including some from the pre-Colgate days at Rubinstein, were brought in to run the company. Within a year, "the grand old lady" was back in the black. As Weiss points out:

> We started to be specialists again. At 300 Park Avenue, they didn't realize that what sells in Paris doesn't work in Brazil. We decentralized more. The company that lost $30 million one year made a profit the next year. It's exciting to take something that's dying and restore it.

Weiss's rescue of Helena Rubinstein mirrors some of the broader trends now transforming the American economy. The explosion of the nation's entrepreneurial sector has coincided with the development of a broad array of smaller firm-oriented financiers, including small banks, commercial finance companies, new investment banks, and venture capital firms. Eschewing the banking by formula that is commonplace among the financial giants, these financiers make their decisions based upon their essentially "seat of the pants" assessment of small firms and their specific market niches.

This trend contrasts sharply with the approach of the last two decades in which size and agglomeration were the fashion. During the great merger waves of the 1960s and 1970s, instead of building new companies the nation's dominant financial institutions encouraged giants such as Colgate to buy up scores of smaller firms.

Between 1963 and 1975, the economy witnessed over 26,500 mergers, and by 1978 the trend reached epidemic proportions with 4,462 consolidations involving over $43 billion in assets. Seeking to accomplish by acquisition what they could not develop internally, some twenty-five of the nation's top 200 companies participated in an astonishing 700 mergers during the period.[1]

But as seen at Rubinstein and Kokomo's Continental Steel, these acquisitions frequently failed to meet expectations. Although the giant-scale industrial firms could easily arrange the financing to purchase firms, the executives soon found themselves trying to manage a staggeringly diverse array of assets, technologies, and markets. "The attempt to commit our resources outside our core area was a disaster," admits one top Colgate official who has helped sell off some thirty-eight acquisitions in recent years. "All we did was weaken our financial picture by trying to run businesses we didn't know much about."

Colgate's experience was not unique among the ranks of major corporate conglomerators. During the early 1970s, for instance, conglomerate stock prices dropped at twice the rate of the other Fortune 500 firms. Acquired firms, despite the infusion of large company expertise and capital, suffered slower growth and greater rates of liquidation than independent firms during this period, according to a recent MIT study.[2]

While most of the criticism of corporate acquisition has come from traditional critics such as the liberal intelligentsia and labor, increasing numbers of top financiers and corporate executives acknowledge that unbridled merger activity often amounts to bad business. As Florida-based securities lawyer Arthur Burck, who has put together hundreds of acquisitions for such giants as Litton Industries, ITT, and Dow Chemical, bitterly told *Fortune*:

> The takeovers by the corporate giants have damaged a great many companies. The acquisitions have weakened or destroyed countless thousands of small and medium-sized businesses that were star performers when they were independent. . . . A company loses its momentum. Key people have left. Employee morale and efficiency have eroded. When workers become part of a sprawling corporate bureaucracy, the identity of "their" company is lost. Productivity suffers. Ill-advised mergers have damaged a whole generation of incipient growth companies.[3]

The views of such men as Burck, and the poor performance records of many mergers and acquisitions, have led to a growing wave of divestitures by major corporations. Many of the top conglomerates of the 1970s—Beatrice Foods, Armco, LTV Corporation, Colgate—have now moved aggressively to sell off unwanted firms, providing new opportunities for entrepreneurially minded financiers. Between 1979 and 1981 the annual number of conglomerate divestitures of over $50 million jumped from 39 to 66, according to the Chicago-based merger and acquisition firm, W. T. Grimm and Co. In 1982 some 13 percent of all divestitures involved transactions of over $100 million, twice the amount in 1979.[4]

As in the case of Rubinstein, many of the firms divested by conglomerate owners soon regain their former entrepreneurial focus. One study by Oppenheimer and Company of the twenty-four largest spin-offs since 1970 found that three-quarters had outperformed the Standard and Poors 400, often by a wide margin. This record of achievement by spin-off companies has attracted the attention of some of the nation's top investment and commercial finance firms, including G. E. Credit, First Boston, Security Pacific Credit Corporation, Carl Marks, Rhode Island's Narragansett Capital and the Foothill Group.[5]

Many of those financiers now actively encourage corporate divestitures as the best way to guarantee improved company performance. These spin-offs are frequently financed through leveraged buyouts in which buyers pay for the purchase of a company with a combination of cash, sellers' credit, and a loan based upon the divested firm's assets. Under new, independent ownership, the company's often deteriorated physical plant is modernized and its operations trimmed.

Perhaps even more important, financiers are increasingly seeking to bring plant managers into ownership roles, injecting the all-important entrepreneurial element into the operation. Between 1980 and 1982 the number of these management buyouts jumped from 47 to 115 and now accounts for 13 percent of all divestitures.[6] Robert Davidoff, partner in Carl Marks and Company, a leading New York investment firm that normally offers management between 20 and 30 percent ownership of a divested firm, notes:

> Entrepreneurs run things leaner. These companies grow better when the managers are on their own. They love it. There's an ability to bring your own people up. There's a feeling of smallness, closeness. You control your own destiny. Your mistakes become your own, your profits are your own. . . . It gives you a chance to get rich without climbing the bureaucratic ladder. It's the spirit that makes things work.

Davidoff's enthusiasm for management buyouts is understandable in light of Carl Marks's tremendous success with divestitures. Through leveraged buyouts, the New York firm has helped finance turnarounds of companies in such diverse fields as carpet-laying tools, steel office products, movie theater chains, and air-conditioning coil makers. From these and other transactions, Marks's has succeeded in earning a return on investment of over 30 percent annually—equal to that of most venture capital firms.

One of Marks's most successful transactions was the 1980 buyout of Grotnes Metalforming Systems, a Chicago-based maker of machine tools. Long a highly profitable firm, Grotnes had continued to make money after being acquired by Chicago-based Inland Steel in 1967. Although its pretax income was in the top quarter of its industry, Inland executives decided Grotnes was "too insignificant" to justify keeping it.

The news that Inland wanted to sell the plant came as a complete shock to Grotnes's 60-year-old president, C. H. Heinz Stettler. A Swiss immigrant, Stettler had devoted twenty-five years of his life to the firm, playing a considerable role in its success. Now faced with the uncertainty of new ownership or even closure of the plant, Stettler and a top Inland executive, John G. Mack, went into partnership with Carl Marks and bought out the firm.

Today Grotnes remains one of the brightest spots in the hard-hit American machine tool industry; even in the middle of the recession, the company had over $10 million in ready cash, allowing management to use the downturn to retool the operation. But perhaps most remarkable of all has been the transformation of the firm and its people. For Heinz Stettler the idea of owning his own firm once seemed impossible.

> A long time ago I had to decide whether or not I would ever own my own business. Then I thought, no, that's not for me. That's not going to be me. . . . But you know, everything that I'd been doing on behalf of Grotnes'—making deals successfully, selling our engineering, making contracts, taking risks— well, I realized that I was acting like an entrepreneur. I realized that I had learned to work that way as a businessman in America. I had been wrong about myself years ago—and it was quite a revelation.[7]

SMALL IS PROFITABLE

The people-oriented approach to finance represented by the Grotnes rescue has deep roots in the nation's economic past. Since the 1790s small, independent banks have played a central role in providing capital for entrepreneurs. In 1832, with the abolition of the Bank of the United States and its central control over credit and currency,[8] these "free banks" created an ideal milieu for the growth of an expansive entrepreneurial economy. Between 1830 and the Civil War, the number of new state banks exploded fivefold to over 1,500. Like entrepreneur-oriented financial institutions today, many of these new banks worked within particular market niches. There were banks for merchants, importers, mechanics, and farmers. They were so specialized that on the island of Nantucket a special institution arose called the Pacific Bank, designed for the primary purpose of financing whaling journeys on an ocean thousands of miles and many months away.[9]

But by the turn of the century, banking, like industry, had fallen increasingly under the spell of giantism. "After 1900, the banking system seemed to split in half," notes banking historian Paul Trescott. "Big banks sought to keep pace with their giant customers." Later, controls applied during the Depression era sharply curtailed the flexibility of the smaller banks while restrictive regulations played into the hands of the largest financial institutions. From 20,000 in 1930, the number of banks had dropped to only 14,000 by 1974. By then, the nation's hundred largest institutions controlled nearly 70 percent of the nation's banking assets.[10]

Today's entrepreneurial ascendancy, however, has created a new surge of small, locally oriented banks. Reversing a half-century-old pattern, small banks began to increase their market share in the late 1970s; by 1982 the number of commercial banks had soared to 14,500. Applications for new federal bank charters jumped from 35 in 1977 to 189 in 1982.[11]

The remarkable renaissance of the nation's small and medium-sized banks, which commit an estimated two-thirds of the credit obtained by small businesses, is reflected in their superior earnings record. In 1981, for instance, banks with under $100 million in assets earned an average return on equity nearly twice that of their multibillion-dollar competitors. Although a higher percentage of small banks lost money, over 28.8 percent of banks with assets under $100 million and 17.7 percent of banks with under $1 billion earned returns in excess of 17 percent, compared to only 13 percent for major banks.[12]

This resurgence points to the persistence of the human factor in the supposedly bloodless profession of banking. In contrast to the giant financial institutions, small banks thrive by establishing intimate ties with local entrepreneurs and communities. For example, Manufacturers' Bank, located in a deteriorating Polish and Hispanic neighborhood of Chicago's northwest side, places special emphasis on the entrepreneurs with whom it does business. "We don't loan off an equation—we look at the people," explains Al Rubens, the bank's ebullient executive vice-president. "We don't lend to corporations. We lend to people who happen to have corporations."

Despite the generally depressed state of its customer base—primarily manufacturers in the wood and wire fabrication field—Manufacturers' Bank is among the most profitable in the nation. Located in an aged brick building on Division Street, Manufacturers' has consistently outperformed its competitors three miles away in the glittering high-rises of Chicago's Loop. In a 1981 survey of 405 Chicago area banks by Crain's Chicago Business, the bank ranked first, with a return on assets of 2.52 percent, a rate more than five times that of multibillion-dollar powerhouses such as Continental Illinois, Harris, and First Chicago.[13]

By lending to people rather than numbers, Manufacturers' avoided many of the disastrous commitments now cutting deeply into the profits of the majors. While the financially sophisticated MBAs from the downtown banks ranged far and wide to make dubious multimillion-dollar loans in the Sunbelt "oil-patch" and overseas, Manufacturers' decidedly less polished salesmen scoured the industrial back alleys of Chicago, serving a customer base painstakingly cultivated since 1911.

"Our customers are people who make things of metal and wood. It's supposed to be part of the economy that's dying but certain people are doing well," Rubens explains, looking rather unbankerlike in his plaid sports jacket. "At this bank we have people with grease under their nails with six-figure bank accounts. They don't wear ties. Sometimes they don't shave, but they know their business." Rubens believes that this concentration on a particular market niche helps Manufacturers' develop the expertise suited to its customers' needs. At the old Chicago bank, aggressive salesmen like Rubens have become intimately familiar with unromantic industries such as nails, wire fasteners, and furniture. This knowledge also helps Manufacturers' loan officers to select their credits more judiciously and develop a permanent base of reliable customers.

But much of Manufacturers' appeal lies simply in its style of doing business. Walking in from the grit and hustle of Division Street, customers are treated wtih the courtesy and intimacy reminiscent of small-town America. Hard-bitten businessmen, elderly Polish ladies, and retired steelworkers come to the bank not only to cash checks and make deposits, but also to chat with their old friends behind the tellers' cages. With over half their 110 employees on staff for more than ten years, some for well over thirty, Manufacturers' offers depositor and borrower alike a sense of continuity rarely found in the highly depersonalized world of the major financial institutions.

A former top executive at the multibillion-dollar Harris Bank downtown, President Fred Sack believes giant financial institutions have lost the ability to deal with small, individual business. The 69-year-old banking veteran notes that the press for ever larger volume loans creates a climate inimical to entrepreneurs. "Here, the entrepreneur can talk to us like family," he asserts. "Compared to the banks downtown, this place is a godsend."

Manufacturers' successful blend of people orientation and small-business lending mirrors some of the broader trends now transforming American finance. Although present in communities across the nation, this new movement is perhaps most pronounced in those areas experiencing spectacular growth in small and medium-sized companies. High-flying Florida, for instance, infused with funds from Latin American and senior citizens, has suddenly emerged into what some observers believe is the nation's hottest financial market.[14] Building upon a base in the small business-minded Cuban community, Raoul Masvidal has built his Biscayne Bank into a burgeoning $600 million institution in just the past decade.

A similar trend toward new banks has taken place in Texas, where during the 1970s the number of banks jumped by some 25 percent, better than two and a half times the national average. Along with Sunbelt rival California, Texas accounted for half the 189 new bank charters granted by the U.S. Controller of the Currency in 1982. In January 1983 over twenty-one new banks opened in the Lone Star State alone; California, with over 327 banking concerns, has another 127 institutions waiting for charters, almost five times the number of applicants back in 1976. Spurred by deregulation, which has allowed broader loan opportunities, the number of new Savings and Loan applications in California jumped from less than five in 1981 to ninety-three in the first *half* of 1983.[15]

Many of these new financial institutions hope to follow Manufacturers' strategic focus on specific local markets. The Bank of New Braunfels, located 30 miles north of San Antonio, has focused heavily on the city's burgeoning tourist and real estate industry and enjoyed an almost 800 percent increase in return on equity between 1977 and 1982. Newly founded Pacific Heritage Bank in Torrance, California, is focusing its efforts on the local Japanese-American community. And in Northern California the new Silicon Valley Bank specializes in financing the growth of venture capital-backed technology firms. Notes Salvador Serrantino, a Santa Monica bank consultant:

> The big ones compete for that segment of the business that doesn't require personal treatment. The public is left with a void as the large institutions feel they must get larger and leave the local market not only unattended but ignored. They feel that there is no way that they can practically serve the markets, so they write them off.[16]

Spurred by the success of entrepreneurial financiers, many large banks no longer "write off" these burgeoning market niches. With the increased deregulation of the industry and the development of interstate banking, some experts expect larger money center banks to challenge smaller institutions in many local markets. One 1983 study conducted by the accounting firm of Arthur Anderson predicts that acquisitions by large institutions could wipe out as many as 40 percent of the nation's small banks, allowing those with over $1 billion in assets to boost their share of the industry's assets from 53 to 65 percent by 1990.[17]

But to succeed in the markets served by small banks, large financial institutions first must develop the sort of human skills so evident at smaller banks like Manufacturers'. While major banks such as Chase Manhattan, Bank of New York, and Crocker National Bank have all recently set up separate units to serve entrepreneurial customers, some top executives remain doubtful that their banks can adapt to the needs of diverse, often highly individualistic entrepreneurs.

"Big banks face a real challenge," says Frederick Hammer, executive vice-president of New York's Chase Manhattan Bank, the nation's third largest. "They have the right kinds of people, big banks don't. [Small banks] have people at the branch level who are generalists, who have both credit and sales skills as well as the versatility necessary to compete in today's environment."[18]

FROM GIANNINI TO GIANTISM

Perhaps no institution more epitomizes American finance's affair with giantism than the nation's largest commercial bank, the Bank of America. Started in San Francisco's colony of Italian immigrants, initially it exemplified the small banking principles still carried out with such fervor at places such as Chicago's Manufacturers'. Yet today, after nearly eight decades of almost unbridled growth, a deeply troubled Bank of America struggles to cope with the price of giant-scale success.

Amadeo Giannini, the bank's founder, rose from almost total obscurity in the years before World War I. At a time when California finance seemed utterly insignificant compared to the titans of Wall Street or the Loop, Giannini was an outsider even within the paltry local establishment of his hometown. His real peers were such unconventional bankers as A. Levy, who took a bank charter in order to finance Ventura County's bean farmers, or Casper Cohen, founder of Los Angeles' Union Bank, whose first function was to store sheepskins for his largest group of customers, Basque sheepherders.

Like Levy and Cohen, Giannini was an outsider who found his first customers among the credit-hungry farmers of California. Under the tutelage of his stern stepfather, "Boss" Scaetana, Giannini learned the vegetable business as a middleman selling to the predominantly Italian and Chinese vegetable peddlers on San Francisco's waterfront. "He was alert to everything and absorbed business like a blotter does ink," Scaetana would later recall. "It was not long after he started coming into the office that I began to get business from people I had never heard about or done business with before."[19]

By his mid-twenties, Giannini's knack for working with small merchants had made him a wealthy man. But for the young Italian-American the lure of business proved irresistible. He moved into real estate and eventually was asked to serve on the board of the local Columbus Building and Loan Society. Almost immediately, Giannini began pressing the board to concentrate on small-scale businesses, a move infuriating to his elders at the Building and Loan. Branded as "too radical," Giannini decided to start his own bank, based on serving the small businesspeople of the city's large Italian community.[20]

Opening its doors on October 17, 1904, the Bank of Italy occupied one room in a North Beach building. With an initial capitalization of $150,000 gathered mostly from friends, the bank was dismissed by the city's haughty banking establishment as just another marginal immigrant business. But within twenty years Giannini built the Bank of Italy into the largest financial institution west of Chicago and, in keeping with its new status, changed its name to Bank of America in the late 1920s.[21]

Key to the bank's explosive growth was Giannini's small business-oriented marketing strategy. Ignoring the conventions of his staid competitors, Giannini became the first banker in California to advertise and make a point of providing personal service to all his customers. As part of his people-oriented credo, Giannini strictly prohibited private offices and even sat at a modest desk on the banking floor himself. Accused by other bankers of lacking dignity, Giannini responded:

> Our job was to make money for the bank. It was not secret that we wanted to make money and make the bank grow, so I cannot see how going after business, as any mercantile firm would do, could be undignified. We took our bank to the people. We placed our branches where the public could see us or talk to us without any rigamarole or red tape. . . . The bank is not a secret enterprise. It is a business and at the same time a public function.[22]

This focus on taking the bank to the people led Giannini to look for new ways of tapping sources of capital. In 1911, for instance, he initiated a passbook savings program for children. By 1928, over 154,000 California schoolchildren, a group larger than the combined contemporary populations of Sacramento and Fresno, held savings accounts of over $7.3 million. In the early 1920s, Giannini also inaugurated a stock purchase plan for employees, the first of its kind in the nation. By the end of the decade, bank employees were its largest single group of shareholders. Giannini explained, "We intend to make them rich, to make the bank so overwhelmingly their first interest that they will not desire outside remuneration."[23]

Initially, Giannini's obsession with the human factor also lay behind his greatest innovation, the development of branch banking. As he traveled throughout the broad outreaches of pre–World War II California, Giannini courted community leaders and hired locally based branch managers, tying the bank closely to literally thousands of small local economies. Major emphasis was placed on winning the support of local worthies in each town with a Bank of America branch. Often Giannini himself would follow a prominent wine grower into his fields, relenting only when he had won his deposit and, frequently, his purchase of bank stock.

But as the bank expanded, Giannini gradually began to lose faith in the entrepreneurial forces so prominent in its growth. Like many of the entrepreneurial giants, Giannini imagined his era to be the last for individualistic enterprise. "The era of small business is past," he declared in 1928. "It is now an era of the merger, big companies, nationwide and worldwide in scope."[24]

The onset of the Depression accelerated the bank's increasing trend toward giantism. In the midst of the 1933 banking crisis, the governor of the San Francisco Federal Reserve Bank, looking at the state of many Bank of America customers, informed Washington that the bank had become "hopelessly insolvent." Panicked and deeply shaken, Giannini was forced to ask for some $38 million in credit from the Reconstruction Finance Corporation as a hedge against possible losses. Under his guiding hand, the bank slowly regained its momentum and by 1945 emerged as the nation's largest.[25]

But with Giannini's retirement that same year, a new generation of leaders who were deeply influenced by the thirties' experience took control of the bank. In the late 1940s and 1950s, these managers forced out the last of Giannini's small business-oriented cronies and imposed a highly conservative, giant-oriented banking philosophy. "[Bank President] Wendt was convinced we were going into another Depression," recalls one senior bank official. "He was a very conservative man and we lost market share and never got it back. Even today, among older people in the bank, there is still a lot of fear from the Depression experience."

Like other leviathans in steel, autos, and electronics, the Bank of America ultimately fell victim to its own giantism. Once tightly rooted in California's enormously diverse entrepreneurial economy, the bank now roamed the world looking for massive loan opportunities with either foreign countries or Fortune 500 giants. Under President Tom Clausen, emphasis shifted toward emulation of the elitist style of its eastern competitors. As Tracy Herrick, a former vice-president at the bank's central San Francisco headquarters, put it:

The bank got to be very snobbish. If you wanted to get any-where you had to be in world banking. You had to be from one of the top four business schools. . . . By 1975, there was no one in the bank who could talk to small business. They couldn't walk the walk, they couldn't talk the talk and make the jokes, which was exactly what Giannini could do. He pushed and promoted. But Clausen was a numbers man, not a customer's man. Hell, he never had a customer.

Throughout the 1970s, this shift toward increasingly large loans seemed both inevitable and inexorable. Under "numbers man" Clausen, the bank's profits reached record levels. While other finan-ciers were risking all on new ventures down in San Jose and south-ern California, pin-striped professionals on Montgomery Street concluded massive deals with representatives of the nation's great corporations and foreign heads of state.

In this milieu, few of the bright, aggressive young executives at the bank saw much point in cultivating the small business loan market. Increasingly, these customers fell to either large competitors or smaller, more entrepreneur-oriented banks or commercial fi-nance companies. Over lunch in the company's executive dining room high above the bank's Los Angeles regional office, bank chairman Lee Prussia explained:

It's more fun to bank GM than an auto parts shop. Entrepre-neurs tend to be oddballs, nonconformists, and they are frowned upon. Bankers are more prone to this because of a ten-dency natural to a big bank. . . . It is much easier for a big bank to deal with big customers. For the Bank of America, it is eas-ier if you deal with big numbers. You have to deal with a credit rating service which makes you feel more comfortable. It's an unknown with smaller business.

By the early 1980s, the Bank of America—with over 1,100 branches, 37,000 employees, and some $118 billion in assets—was the polar opposite of the small business-oriented institution born in the vegetable markets of San Jose and San Francisco. In the words of the *Wall Street Journal,* the bank had become "as well known for its resistance to change as for its enormous size."[26] In 1981, the Bank suffered a humiliating 31-percent decline in profits, the largest setback in nearly two decades. At the same time, its once highly regarded foreign loans became more of an embarrassment. Although not as exposed as most of its New York–based rivals, Bank of America groaned under the weight of dubious transactions such as its $2.5 billion in loans to economically distressed Mexico.[27]

Chastened by these setbacks, Prussia—who invests *his* private capital in a fund specializing in small and medium-sized firms—and new president Sam Armacost have now adopted a marketing strategy reminiscent of Giannini himself. Deemphasizing the importance of foreign and other large-ticket loans, the Bank has opened a concerted drive to reestablish its once strong links to California's entrepreneurial firms. Already a fierce marketing drive has helped establish its leading position as prime leasing agency for venture-backed deals in the Silicon Valley. Armacost promises more of the same: "The Bank of America got fat and lazy at a time when it should have been screwing down and going for the throat. . . . We want people who can execute. If they can't, we'll execute them."[28]

THE LOW-FAT BANKERS

While the executives at Bank of America and other major financial institutions across the country were concerning themselves with the intricacies of high finance, Don Valentine was placing his bets on a host of California's tiny technology start-up companies. By providing equity financing to new start-ups and young firms that often couldn't get the money anywhere else, Valentine and other venture capitalists have sparked many spectacular successes including Apple

Computers, Federal Express, Prime Computers, and Tandem. In less than a decade they have transformed venture capital from a nearly moribund industry into a $1.4 billion juggernaut, financing nearly 1,750 companies across the country.[29]

Like Amadeo Giannini, Valentine and many other top venture capitalists emerged from outside the ranks of the established financial community. Fifteen years ago Valentine was helping build one of the most dynamic electronics companies in America, and getting bored in the process. As director of marketing at National Semiconductor, he felt increasingly at odds with the company's swelling corporate bureaucracy. Having participated in the firm's early days, when he and company president Charles Spork threw dice against the wall of their empty building, he sensed that perhaps his greatest entrepreneurial triumph was behind him.

"That's why I went into the venture business," Valentine explains, relaxing comfortably in a plaid shirt, his brown boots perched upon his office desk. He gestures toward the movie poster on the wall—Butch Cassidy and the Sundance Kid, his favorite western heroes. "There's still something very special about a company when it's small. That's when the spirit of the *individual* is really prevalent. The fun level is terrific—and I don't do things that aren't fun."

To Don Valentine, the son of a Yonkers teamsters' official, "fun" equals working long hours to find those few small high-technology companies that might grow into tomorrow's National Semiconductor or even the 21st century's IBM. Since 1973, working out of a modest Menlo Park office just up the road from Stanford University, Valentine's Capital Management Services has raised over $70 million in investment capital and helped launch some of the nation's most successful new companies, including Atari, Apple, Pizza Time Theater, and Altos Computers. Over the past ten years Valentine's investments have grown at more than 50 percent compounded annually—sensational even by venture capital standards.

Valentine owes his success not to his dexterity with numbers but to his unique ability to judge people and markets, skills developed over two decades as a marketing manager for both National and Fairchild Semiconductor. Valentine boasts:

I have no training in finance. It's common for people trained in finance to focus on the wrong things. They look at the numbers. People, productivity, markets are all that matter. These MBAs are good at analyzing numbers like those at General Motors, but how do you find the numbers for the product that does not exist? The quest is to perceive radical changes and solutions to existing problems—the investors must foresee the development of a major industry where nothing existed before.

Unlike the large commercial bnaks, which are frequently disdainful of small firms, venture capitalists such as Valentine make their returns by focusing on those few outstanding new companies with the potential for high growth. Although extremely risky, venture capital investments during the last twenty years have earned a remarkable average annual return of 25 percent.[30] Between 1972 and 1979, investment in venture-based public companies rose in value by 224.1 percent compared to a paltry 6.2 percent rise in the blue chip-oriented Value-Line Composite.[31] So spectacular has been venture capital's success that such traditionally conservative financial sources as pension funds have poured almost $200 million annually into venture firms. By 1980, pension funds—including those of such prominent firms as Armco, Alcoa, Chrysler, and General Electric—constituted the largest single investors in venture funds.[32]

This shift toward venture capital illustrates a growing awareness in the financial community of the importance of new companies and the entrepreneurial financiers who best understand them. Unlike the MBA at a large commercial bank, tied to his computer in a high-rise office, Valentine can offer more than money. His greatest asset, he believes, is his "intelligence equity," his unique understanding of high-technology management and markets. Sometimes Valentine helps his companies simply by bringing in the right man for a particular assignment. At Apple Computers, for example, he brought in his close friend and former Intel executive Mike Markkula to serve as president of the fledgling firm, which was started by "the two Steves"—neophyte entrepreneurs Wozniak and Jobs. Valentine believed Markkula's experience would compensate for the founders' lack of management know-how. "Don called me up and said there were two guys in a garage I might want to meet," Markkula recalls. "It's turned out to be a very rewarding piece of matchmaking, both personally and financially."

But often Valentine himself plays a leading management role. Known from his days at National Semiconductor as a harsh but brilliant taskmaster, Valentine attracts entrepreneurs not so much by his money but by their desire for his guiding hand. When he first met Valentine, Altos Computers president Dave Jackson was amazed by his profound grasp of the crowded business computer field and his almost uncanny feel for Altos's proper niche. Jackson was so impressed that he allowed Valentine to shape both Altos's financial and marketing divisions. Now chairman of the board, Valentine is widely credited along with Jackson for turning Altos from a fledgling $8 million company in 1979 into a public firm with well over $74 million in sales three years later. "I needed a strategist and Don's a great one," recalls Jackson, whose investment in Altos soared to over $151.6 million after the public offering.[33] "He's no witch doctor but you tell him a problem and he sets the guidelines for you so you can get a solution. Best of all, he tells me when I'm being an ass."

But despite his own contributions, Valentine insists it is the entrepreneur who stands at the heart of the process. Essentially, Valentine's greatest skill may not be marketing or his contacts. His success stems largely from his recognition of the human factor, his ability to choose that special individual or team of individuals capable of building a superlative company. As Valentine explains:

> We don't invest in any companies where we have doubts about the people. They must have leaders with a commanding presence, self-confident to the point of arrogance. I like people who,

when you ask how big a company they want, say $500 million. I'm looking for some guy who wants a net worth of $50 million. That is the guy who will leap tall buildings in a single bound and stop speeding bullets. We make our money on big, big dreams.

As a nation built upon "big, big dreams," America has always had its venture capitalists. From the British investors' financing of the Jamestown and Plymouth settlements to the venture firms of today, a steady procession of risk-taking financiers bankrolled America's continuous revolution. In the age of railroads, the investors included Cornelius Vanderbilt and E. H. Harriman; in steel, Frick and Morgan; in automobiles, DuPont.

But with the disclosures of the Progressive era and later the catastrophes of the Depression, government regulation increasingly restricted this sort of financial empire-building. With banks under strict control, industrial investment became institutionalized through the public markets and established brokerage firms. By the end of World War II, only the very richest families, among them the Whitneys and the Rockefellers, could afford to dabble in the venture game. Even today, with venture firms bulging with pension funds and other institutional sources, the Hillman Company, run by heirs of a 19th-century Pittsburgh coal magnate, remains the nation's largest venture firm.[34]

These few adventurous hierarchs, however, could not dispel the general atmosphere of conservatism that long afflicted many of the nation's top financial institutions. Up until the late 1970s, major San Francisco banks and financiers generally disdained the entrepreneurs of the Silicon Valley, preferring the safety of more traditional industries such as agribusiness, real estate, and defense. In the early 1950s, few members of such elite groups as the Pacific Union Club took entrepreneurs like Bill Hewlett and David Packard seriously. Peter Bancroft, now managing director of New York's Bessemer Securities and an early investor in Bay Area high-tech firms, recalls:

I think that many of them [the San Francisco elite] thought that entrepreneurship and venture capital wasn't very dignified. I remember one elderly gentleman wanting to know why I was bothering to be involved with those young companies down on the peninsula. . . . There was a real lack of appreciation of what was happening right under their noses.

In the face of such attitudes, the Bay Area's venture capital community developed largely outside the institutions of the San Francisco financial establishment. Often the key players were such rising young executives as Bancroft and Reid Dennis, investing on a highly ad hoc and informal basis. A young executive at Fireman's Fund insurance in San Francisco, Dennis was drawn to venture capital in part because of a rather unique piece of family history. Dennis's grandfather once turned down a young businessman seeking $10,000 to start a new tire company. The young man, whose name was Harvey Firestone, found backing elsewhere and went on to build one of the nation's most important tire firms. "This," Dennis remarks wryly, "made a great impression on me."

Shortly after graduation from Stanford Business School, Dennis was approached by a friend about a young company named Ampex. Not wishing to miss his chance, Dennis invested nearly his entire net worth of $15,000 on the fledgling manufacturer of magnetic tape. After making over $1 million with that small investment, Dennis decided to start what he calls "my double life." Working during the day at a "straight job" at Fireman, he met with friends during lunch breaks and weekends to invest in small, high-tech firms such as American Microsystems and Measurex. Now a full-time venture capitalist, Dennis explains: "[Fireman's Fund] wouldn't touch those companies with a ten-foot pole."

While Dennis and his friends were making deals over lunch, the model for today's venture firm was first taking shape across the country in Boston. Started in 1946, American Research and Development piloted the sort of technology-oriented, high-risk investment strategy that would serve as a model for the rest of the venture industry. Under the leadership of Georges Doriot and with the support of such financiers as Merrill Griswold of the Massachusetts Investors' Trust, ARD sought out technical and entrepreneurial talent throughout the New England area.

After several years of losses, ARD started to make money consistently in 1955. Perhaps its most spectacular success came in 1957 when Doriot invested in a fledgling company named Digital Equipment Corporation. Started in an old woolen mill in the Boston suburb of Maynard, Digital and its founders, Ken Olsen and Harlan Anderson, were nursed along with some $70,000 from ARD; by 1971 that investment was worth a remarkable $350 million. Deeply committed to his firms—Doriot called them his "children"—ARD served not only as financier but as advisor and confidante to the entrepreneurs running them. As Doriot later told *Fortune*'s Gene Bylinsky:

> When you have a child, you don't ask what return you expect. Of course, you have hopes—you hope your child will become President of the United States. But that is not very probable, and if a man is good and loyal and does not achieve a so-called good rate of return, I will stay with him. Some people don't become geniuses until after they are twenty-four, you know. If I were a speculator, the question of return would apply. But I don't consider a speculator—in my definition of the word— constructive. I am building men and companies.[35]

This uniquely personal approach to finance as a process of "building men and companies" helped earn ARD's investors a compounded rate of return of over 15 percent throughout the low inflation decades of the 1950s and 1960s. But with the takeover of the investment firm by the Textron conglomerate in 1971, ARD soon lost its entrepreneurial edge. In the late 1970s and early '80s, when other venture firms were achieving annual returns in the 20- to 40-percent range, conglomeratized ARD experienced returns as embarrassingly low as 3 to 4 percent.[36]

But if ARD is no longer the industry leader, the Doriot tradition of service to entrepreneurs lives on in a whole new generation of venture capitalists. Often experienced entrepreneurs and managers themselves, these venture capitalists have repeatedly proven their ability to spot investment opportunities that would escape most traditional financiers.

In 1969, for instance, Burgess Jamieson first heard about a team of four former IBM executives trying to start a compatible disk drive business in Boulder, Colorado, then little more than a ski resort. Traveling out largely on a hunch, Jamieson, an MIT-trained electrical engineer and former top Honeywell executive, visited Storage Technologies at their "headquarters" in an abandoned supermarket. Hardly noticing the uncarpeted floor, or the lack of private offices, Jamieson was excited by the founders' technology and the future of their marketplace:

When I visited Storage Technologies for the first time, it was four engineers and a bunch of support personnel in an abandoned supermarket. But it was clear that they knew what they were doing. A banker would have looked at them and laughed. I invested.

Fourteen years later, Jamieson's initial $400,000 investment was worth in excess of $40 million as Storage Technologies has emerged as a giant in its field. "Most bankers are used to dealing with tangibles. They look at balance sheet and numbers. But in the computer business you make the decisions on intangibles—a diagram of a computer you can draw on paper but isn't real yet," the veteran venture capitalist explains. "The bank doesn't understand the technology or the people—they are too into the numbers."

With many of the venture capital's most spectacular successes— and some 63 percent of all venture funds[37]—invested in high-technology electronics, Jamieson and other top venture executives fear that the field for such products as microcomputers and disk drives may soon be sated. Increasingly, leading venture capitalists are looking toward new product areas in fields including restaurants, communications, and consumer products for the next decade's investments.

John Hines, president of Continental Illinois Ventures, has demonstrated the wisdom of such diversification with his many highly successful investments in firms involved in widely ranging fields from contraceptives and graphic packaging to real estate, oil, and cable television. To Hines, many recent entrants into the venture community are already falling into the trap of making investments based purely on technological considerations, not on the quality of the entrepreneurial talent. "I get these little squirts in here with their computers. They say this technology will get 38.8 percent return but they can't go inside someone's office without a computer in their belts," the venture capitalist growls in his downtown Chicago office. "You don't need a computer. You look at the people and the markets—that's what makes the business go."

The success of Hines and other people-oriented venture capitalists has begun to transform the thinking in even the most traditional financial institutions. Not only are banks such as the Bank of America and Wells Fargo making determined efforts to lend money to young, start-up firms, but venture capital's success has helped produce a whole new breed of high-powered executives within investment banking, long the most conservative bastion of the financial establishment.

Indeed, the last decade has seen the emergence of a whole host of new or previously obscure underwriters oriented to serving the equity needs of entrepreneurial companies. Much of this activity has taken place in San Francisco, where young firms such as Robertson, Colman, Stephens, Montgomery Securities, Hambrecht and Quist have become major players in recent years. But even staid Wall Street's pecking order has been affected by the entrepreneurial explosion, which has sparked the emergence of such investment banking companies as L. F. Rothschild, Unterberg, and Tobin. Close to the venture community, these firms have risen to prominence by bringing to the public market such new issues as Televideo, Gulfstream, and Apollo Computers, each with early market valuations well in excess of $1 billion. Since 1980, the number of new issues has more than doubled to over 1,200 annually, some garnering as much as 100 times earnings in the public marketplace.[38]

Due largely to this spectacular explosion of new issues, these underwriters have begun to shift even mainstream Wall Street away from its preoccupation with the Fortune 500 giants and toward the developing entrepreneurial configuration. Seizing this new marketplace has been a central strategy in the resurgence of firms such as Ladenburg Thalmann, a medium-sized Wall Street investment house founded in 1876. Once floundering, under the guiding hand of president Stephen Weisglass, Ladenburg Thalmann has thrived even as most other smaller houses were swallowed up by Merrill Lynch and other giants. Weisglass, whose firm has invested in such fast-growing companies as Cambridge Bioscience Corporation and Computer Memories Inc., explains:

We try not to compete with the First Bostons and Merrill Lynches of the world. Our market niche is the emerging growth company and the entrepreneur. We feel very strongly that the strength of this country is the emerging, young, individualistic type of people who want to go out and build a business or a company or a service on an idea.

Closely tied to the venture community, many of these emerging investment banking firms espouse the bare-bones approach of Don Valentine rather than the traditional formulas of investment banking. Montgomery Securities, prominent in the underwriting of such growth issues as Systems Industries, traditionally finishes close to the top in intercorporate track meets between California firms. Thom Weisel, the 42-year-old managing director and founder of the firm, is a championship skier who openly prefers to hire highly competitive former athletes than the academic superstars recruited by the leading eastern houses. "If you can do a good quarter mile, you're hired," jokes one Montgomery analyst. "The people here would die at Shearson."

Perhaps more important, Montgomery sees itself as a participant in a new economy. There's little attempt to maintain the distance from the marketplace cultivated by the numbers-oriented investment houses. Instead everyone—including managing partner Weisel—throws himself into his work with the enthusiasm and risk-oriented attitude of a venture capitalist. Like Giannini, who occupied a building on the same block fifty years earlier, Weisel eschews the imperial trappings of many of his eastern counterparts—at least in the office. Often arriving before five in the morning, the trim banker spends much of his time on the trading floor with his brokers and analysts. Amid the screaming and clamor of the firm's trading floor, Weisel remarked:

> We're one step from venture capital. We want you to take the same attitude you take in slalom race. If you can't make it, I don't want to see you around here. . . . There are no salesmen here with fancy private offices. We want our people on the firing line—all the time.

6

AMERICA
AS NUMBER ONE

Shunji Shinoda was brought up to be the model Japanese corporate man. Upon graduation from the elite Tokyo University in 1955, he immediately went to work for Obayashi-gumi, Japan's fifth largest construction company. With traditional stoicism, he accepted the company's assignments throughout Japan and Latin America that kept him constantly away from his wife and children.

Then in 1972 came Shinoda's big break. At the comparatively young age of 42, he was appointed president of the newly formed $4 million Obayashi-America corporation. Within eight years, the energetic executive built hotels, industrial parks, and office buildings across the Pacific states, increasing company revenues to over $70 million. Yet as Obayashi-America grew, Shinoda's conflicts with the Tokyo home office intensified; many top executives resented his increasingly American style of doing business—quick, to the point, and without elaborate courtesies.

Angered at his refusal to work within the "consensus" style of management, Shinoda's bosses ordered him back to Tokyo in 1980. Utterly frustrated, the then 50-year-old executive felt he had no alternative but to do the unthinkable—leave the secure womb of Obayashi and start his own business. Shinoda, whose delicate features contrast with hands roughened over three decades in the construction trade, recalls:

I had been thinking of staying longer and building an empire here. I am like a rocket and they wanted me to stop. My friends are here, my family likes it. I like the American way of doing things. In a word, Japanese society is one big bureaucracy, one big pyramid. Here it's different; there's risk, but it's not gloomy all the time. You can make your own future.

At a time when many Americans fear the nation is slouching toward an inevitable decline, newcomers like Shunji Shinoda testify to the enduring appeal of its basic individualistic ethos. Flooding the borders in numbers not seen since the great immigrant waves of the early 1900s, legal immigrants over the past decade have more than doubled to over 800,000 annually; as many as a half million more have entered illegally.[1]

These new immigrants—more than 80 percent from Asia or Latin America—follow the path trodden by earlier waves from Europe, and are transforming not only their own lives, but also the communities in which they settle. Before Shinoda and other Japanese immigrants started arriving in the late 1960s, for instance, Los Angeles' Little Tokyo district was only an extension of Skid Row, a bleak and rapidly deteriorating district. Today, aided by infusions of overseas capital and the entrepreneurial skills of new immigrants like Shinoda, the district sparkles with new buildings, theaters, and restaurants.

Like the original *Issei*, the first-generation Japanese who first settled Little Tokyo, Shinoda struggled mightily to establish himself in the United States. Shunned by his former employees, Shinoda had to seek out clients among the 8,000 "new Issei"—from sushi chefs to independent traders—who have migrated to Los Angeles in recent years.[2] With a handful of contracts from his fellow immigrant businessmen, in late 1980 Shinoda opened his Taiyo Construction Company in a run-down hotel several miles west of downtown.

Working virtually alone, he took direct charge of even the most intricate details of each project, assuring that his buildings would be of the highest quality. Taiyo's reputation for low cost and top grade work soon spread throughout the Asian community; working often until midnight, Shinoda almost always finished his work on time, an essential factor for his predominantly small business clientele. By late 1981, the hard work started to pay off. Billing over $800,000 that year, Taiyo steadily expanded until its 1983 revenues exceeded $3 million. Even now, in his austere new office just outside the Little Tokyo district, Shinoda professes amazement at his successful change from corporate manager to entrepreneur, a transformation made in America:

> You know, when I left my company I was really scared. I had my salary check every week for twenty-six years. I'm over 50 and no one my age would try starting his own company in Japan. . . . But after all that time, I wanted a piece. I mean, why should Mr. Obayashi or someone else get all the benefit of my skill? In Japan, there'd be no way out, but this is still a fabulous country.

Shunji Shinoda's success reflects the fact that the United States still remains the world's great bastion for entrepreneurship. Whole sections of central Los Angeles have been transformed into bustling small business centers by the expanding and highly entrepreneurial Korean community, which boasts a rate of new business formation more than twice the average for the rest of the population,[3] and which has turned a once desolate, sprawling urban jungle into a thriving commercial center. Indeed, throughout California from San Diego to San Francisco, immigrants from such varied lands as Vietnam, Thailand, and Mexico have supplied both muscle and entrepreneurial drive for sectors as diverse as restaurants and high-technology electronics.

Like California, Southern Florida also has benefited greatly from the new immigrant wave. Spurred by its large Cuban population, in recent years the Miami area has emerged from a resort economy to become the financial and trade capital of Latin America. Tripling in population since 1955, Miami and surrounding Dade County now boast over fifty-five foreign-owned banks, the most in the country, and have enjoyed an infusion of over $3 billion in the past decade from Latin American investors. "A lot of people attribute the fantastic growth of this city to the jet engine, air-conditioning, and Fidel Castro," remarks Sandy Lane, a director of the local Chamber of Commerce.[4]

Nor do the immigrant entrepreneurs flock only to the cities of the ascendant Sunbelt. In New York, immigrants from such countries as India and Korea have helped stabilize scores of urban neighborhoods by opening corner groceries, fruit stands, and other small businesses. Other newcomers, including immigrants from the Middle East, China, and Puerto Rico, have played a major role in reversing the decline of the city's fabled garment district, according to studies conducted by the New York-based Population Council.[5]

Like the Irish and Italians of the 19th century, most immigrants today start off at the lower rungs, working at menial jobs few Americans would be willing to accept. Yet despite their lowly origins and often debilitating lack of language skills, foreign-born Americans, according to recent studies, have displayed a flair for entrepreneurship equal to or above that of the native born. Due largely to this entrepreneurial activity, after ten years new immigrants boast income levels—and a tax burden—higher than native-born Americans, according to a 1982 Congressional study. "The average immigrant," concluded the report's coauthor, University of Illinois economist Julian L. Simon, "is a remarkably good investment for taxpayers. . . . [He] is not heavily on welfare or unemployment compensation rolls as popular wisdom has it."[6]

The immigrant contribution extends even into the most advanced sectors of the American economy. Engineers from overseas include some of the nation's most important high-technology entrepreneurs, led by such high-flyers as Korea's Phil Huang, founder of $1 billion Televideo, Indian Jugi Tandon, scion of the highly successful Tandon computer disk drive firm, and British-born Dave Jackson, founder of fast-growing Altos Computers. Foreign engineers have played so crucial a role in America's high-technology industries that attempts to restrict their entry into the nation's schools have elicited strong opposition by one of the most important electronics organizations, the American Electronics Association.

More than anything else, these immigrants are perhaps the best guarantors that America's continuous revolution—producing new firms and innovations—will persist into the next century. Many, like Israeli Joe Nakash, came to the United States virtually penniless. For his first few days after arriving in New York in 1962, Nakash spent his evenings on the subways. Twenty years later, the Israeli founder of Jordache Jeans is a multimillionaire and prominent figure in New York's fashion revival. "In Israel, it was a big thing for me to think I could be a driver for a rich man," Nakash recalls. "But when I came to America, I saw it was possible to be a rich man."[7]

This almost magical regard for America's possibilities, often dismissed as naive by sophisticated observers, captivates not only successful immigrants, but also millions of people in countries scattered across the world. By a margin better than two to one, according to one 1983 survey, foreigners from Europe, Japan, and Latin America believe the influence of the United States will grow in coming decades.[8] To most, the country still represents the vanguard of the new—in technology, in culture, in lifestyles.

Their growing faith in the American economy stems largely from the dynamism of its emerging entrepreneurial sector. Although such industries as autos and steel have slipped in the United States as elsewhere, the nation's emerging companies have helped America to continue its domination of cutting-edge industries such as biotechnology and microelectronics, the latter an industry destined to be the world's largest by the 1990s according to the Worldwatch Institute. Despite determined European and Japanese efforts, American entrepreneur-driven technology firms produced 63 percent of the world's semiconductors in 1982.[9]

This technological power, plus enormous agricultural and other natural resources, has not escaped the attention of key corporations overseas. Since 1973 foreign investment in the United States has jumped by an annual rate of over 18 percent, reaching $65.5 billion in 1980.[10] The bulk of these investments has come from America's leading industrial competitors, many of whom realize the nation's importance as the shaper of the economic future. By the late 1970s, West Germans—once among the leading recipients of American dollars—started investing over $1 billion annually across the Atlantic, more than twice the U.S.'s new investment in Germany. Many major purchases have been made in the stock of such young high-technology firms as Advanced Micro-Devices, American Micro-Systems, and Litronix. As the business magazine *German International* observes, "In contrast to the Federal Republic, not to say the whole of the EEC [European Economic Community], America has again become the land of opportunity."[11]

But perhaps most telling of all has been the rapidly growing investment in America's economy by Japan, our most aggressive and tenacious competitor. Long interested in the nation's prodigious food and energy resources, Japanese firms have stepped up their investment activity in industrial fields as diverse as electronics, steel, and automobiles. Between 1973 and 1980, Japanese direct investment grew from a mere $152 million to over $4.2 billion, an almost 28-percent increase.

Although some of this can be attributed to attempts to stem protectionist sentiments, most Japanese firms, according to Japanese government studies, invest primarily to tap America's large markets and learn from the entrepreneurial technology and service firms now shaping the economic future of the planet. Eager to tap the innovative brilliance of these firms, Japanese electronics giants such as Fujitsu and Hitachi have entered into co-ventures with such firms as Amdahl and National Semiconductor; one of Japan's leading bio-technology firms, Green Cross, does much of its key research in tandem with such American entrepreneurial companies as Hana Biologics, Collaborative Research, and Genex.[12] In the mind of many top Japanese executives, these young companies, along with such superbly run large firms as IBM, constitute the advance guard of the new economic era. One top Japanese executive, Takashi Sakai, executive vice-president of C. Itoh America, observes pointedly:

No place else do you see these new ventures and technologies. There's a sense of a limitlessness, of opportunity that we cannot have in Japan, crowded in our island, or in Europe. You have the natural treasures, the people, and the technologies—you just need to learn how to utilize them.

THE AGE OF THE PESSIMISTS

Perhaps the people most pessimistic about America today are Americans themselves. Over the last few decades America's once robust self-confidence has steadily eroded. Between 1963 and 1977, according to the Gallup Poll, Americans' confidence in their future dipped from 64 percent to 41 percent. By 1983, nearly 83 percent viewed the coming years as ones of "downward expectations," according to one survey.[13]

The reasons for this distressing loss of faith are numerous and widespread. High interest rates have placed the goal of home ownership out of sight for millions of supposedly middle-class Americans; continually escalating rates of unemployment have caused many, especially the young, to doubt their own future prospects; the failures of the nation's political leadership, particularly the Vietnam debacle and Watergate, greatly reduced faith in basic institutions— between 1966 and 1979 the public's approval of Congress and the executive branch dropped to well under 20 percent.[14]

But perhaps most devastating of all has been the perceptible decline in economic strength of the United States since the onset of the 1960s. Since 1963 Americans have lost markets in such diverse products as automobiles, electronic and agricultural machinery, pharmaceuticals, and telecommunications equipment. Indeed, during the last two decades America's economic growth rate has been among the lowest in the industrialized world, less than half that of Japan and well below that of most European industrial nations.[15]

Caught largely by surprise by this weak economic performance, America's top business, labor, and political leaders seem to have lost faith in the nation's future. A 1982 survey of 142 leaders by the

Yankelovich organization revealed that the vast majority expected the nation to lose increasing market share in a range of industries from consumer electronics to automobiles and steel. About the future competitiveness of twenty-five major industries, the leaders surveyed expressed strong confidence in only ten. America's current leaders, Yankelovich concluded:

> . . . betray a psychology of self-effacement—a lack of surefootedness on the part of many who will be the prime architects of the American response to the Japanese. . . . There seems to be a potential danger of our leaders being trapped by a self-fulfilling prophecy.[16]

Convinced the nation is slipping, many top figures from the world of business, government, and academia believe the road to national salvation lies in some form of moral rearmament. Nearly two-thirds of all the top business officials in the Yankelovich survey named "focus on self" as one of the leading causes of America's economic problems. Some observers, among them George Gilder, believe that America's decline is in fact a symptom of American "spiritual decay"; he and other fundamentalist conservatives see salvation only in a return to the traditional male-dominated moralism of the 19th century.[17] They are anxious to impose on everyone archaic puritan values shared by a small minority of Americans, and they virtually ignore the deeply antiauthoritarian roots of the current entrepreneurial revolution, including the increasing prominence of women in the business world.

The current pessimism also expresses itself in less quaint but equally disturbing ways. Locked within a cycle of despair and self-deprecation, many influential Americans seem prepared to abandon our individualistic entrepreneurial values for the centrally controlled economic approaches taken in recent years in such countries as Japan, West Germany, and France. Harvard's Ezra Vogel, a leading academic, has openly stated that Americans need to leave their individualistic impulses behind and embrace the "communitarian" structures of our bureaucratically-directed competitors. In his brilliant if disturbing polemic *Japan as Number One*, Vogel writes:

America's institutions are not strong enough to guide these developments or to respond effectively to the problems of [the nation's] decreasing economic competitiveness. . . . Japan, with its greater sense of group orientation, more recent emergence from feudalism, and government-led modernization has developed solutions for these problems that America, with its more individualistic and legalistic history, might never have invented.[18]

Convinced of Japan's superiority, Vogel sees America's salvation in embracing a "more central leadership" patterned on the domination by government and giant corporate bureaucracies that is characteristic of Japan and many other nations. Like other advocates of "communitarian" values such as George Cabot Lodge and Robert Reich, Vogel urges the creation of an elite corps of government bureaucrats, like those in Japan's Ministry of International Trade and Industry, to work out the nation's basic industrial policy. Although Vogel admits such systems work primarily under control of giant institutions, in his opinion they have the virtue of avoiding the "haphazard" competition characteristic of America's entrepreneurial economy.[19]

Obsessed with foreign models, Vogel and others of like mind largely ignore the creative role of entrepreneurs in the revival of America's industrial greatness. Robert Reich, for instance, hails the confluence of giant institutions in France, Japan, and West Germany for helping "enhance the creation of wealth." Comparing the performance of American and foreign steelmakers, Reich praises government-backed programs abroad that assist the competitiveness of major industrial firms and he suggests America adopt a similar industrial policy. Instead of the traditional ethos of individualism and competition, he describes major corporations as the designated "agents of society" who must work in close conjunction with elite bureaucrats to determine national economic policies.[20]

Fixated on the failures of America's giants, Reich and other advocates of foreign-style government intervention seem utterly oblivious to the massive entrepreneurial transformation of the last decade. In his discussions of high technology and steel, for instance, the innovative models of venture capital-backed small high-tech firms and steel mini-mills receive little consideration. Reich prescribes more government intervention and "more flexible" corporations as the cure for our persistent economic maladies. He echoes the notion first proposed in more elegant fashion by John Kenneth Galbraith some two decades ago that the large organizations are the prime forums for industrial innovation. There is little room for garage tinkerers and entrepreneurial adventurers in his highly structured world view:

> It is becoming clear that America's economic future depends less on lonely geniuses and backyard inventors than on versatile organizations. . . . The kinds of productive systems that will sustain America's future prosperity are technically intricate. They demand an exacting degree of teamwork.[21]

In its most extreme form, this corporatist view expresses itself in the call for the formation of a multibillion-dollar federal loan board, based on the Depression-era RFC. Like the original model, this board would dispense funds to industries and companies deemed socially or economically essential. Such an approach would also tend to favor large-scale units, such as giant steel or semiconductor firms. As one longtime Washington hand, Senator William Proxmire, points out:

> Money will go where the political power is. It will go where the union power is mobilized. . . . It will go where the mayors and governors, as well as congressmen and senators, have the power to push it. Anyone who thinks government funds will be allo-

cated to firms according to merit has not lived or served in
Washington very long.[22]

While some are convinced the nation's future economic health
demands control by powerful and unelected new institutions, other
pessimists frankly assert it is time to give up the struggle for world
industrial leadership. To them, the United States is rapidly becoming a "post-industrial" nation, whose interests now lie with maintaining the current social equilibrium. As Paul Blumberg, professor
of sociology at New York's City University sees it: "I think we're
witnessing the Europeanization of the American class structure—a
combination of declining living standards, increasing inequality,
and lower social mobility."[23]

Such a "Europeanization" even has its advocates among America's intellectual elite, who openly believe our nation should turn
away from the production of goods and embrace the sort of relaxed
attitude toward the competitive struggle characteristic of the last
half century of the British empire. Looking back across the Atlantic,
respected observers such as John Kenneth Galbraith, Anthony
Lewis, and Andrew Hacker have argued in defense of what Galbraith calls a "more leisurely relationship with industrial life."[24] In
perhaps the most chilling of the pessimistic accounts, the critically
acclaimed *The End of the American Era*, Hacker argues:

[the] option for Americans is to acknowledge candidly that we
are no longer capable of being a great power. A majority of us
would have to admit that our nation is in a stage of moral en-
ervation; that we have no more lessons to impart to others; that
the way of life we have created has ceased to be a model for
people beyond our borders. . . . This sort of abdication is by no
means unprecedented; virtually every European nation has re-
linquished its role as a world power and is now content to at-
tend to ordering its domestic arrangements. There is much to
be said for being a Denmark or a Sweden, even a Great Britain
or France or Italy.[25]

THE RISE AND DECLINE OF EUROPE

Americans come by their fascination with Europe naturally. The society, politics, and basic economic system of the United States were forged in the fires of the European experience. To a great extent, Americans are the inheritors of Europe's continuous revolution; long after most European nations have moved away from the entrepreneurism and the forging of new horizons, Americans seek to expand the great experiment in individual self-determination instigated by the Europeans centuries ago.

Modern capitalism emerged during the Renaissance as new ideas overcame tradition and superstition in North and Central Italy and as commercial entrepreneurs replaced the tired feudal elite. "The rugged individualism of Galileo," maintained Schumpeter, "was the individualism of the rising capitalism."[26] But superior science and technology did not guarantee the ascendancy of the new commercial centers; virtually every major innovation of Renaissance and early modern Europe—including gunpowder, paper, printing, and the compass—originated in other lands. More than anything else, it was the human factor, the European zest to exploit and improve the inventions of others, that sparked the new capitalist era.[27]

Nowhere was this new venturesome spirit so profound as in the British Isles. By the 18th century, the industrious English middle class was not only chafing against the aristocratic stranglehold on wealth and power, but it was also creating whole new ways of making and selling goods. "The age is running mad after innovation," quipped Samuel Johnson. "All the business of the world is to be done in a new way; men are to be hanged in a new way; Tyburn itself is not free from the fury of innovation."[28]

This "fury of innovation" brought to prominence new players from outside the entrenched social order. Dissenters, Scotsmen, and Quakers, excluded from the tightly knit Anglican establishment, were at the fore in the launching of the Industrial Revolution. James Watt, the inventor of the steam engine, was a Baptist from Scotland; Richard Arkwright, a barber by trade, became the greatest of the cotton-spinning entrepreneurs; schoolmaster Samuel Walker emerged as the premier ironmaster of northern Britain. At this time, observes British historian T. S. Ashton, "vertical mobility had reached a degree higher than that of any earlier, or perhaps any succeeding, age."[29]

As in high-tech centers today, great progress relied on the interplay of numerous innovators and entrepreneurs; prodded by the fires of competition, industrialists used the steam engine, the iron rail, and the spinning jenny to transform Britain into the first bastion of industrial capitalism. By the mid-1800s British trade volume was almost twice that of France, its nearest competitor. "The workshop of the world" produced a full half of the world's total supply of pig iron and dominated virtually every industrial sector.[30]

America inherited England's entrepreneurial spirit and soon surpassed the performance of the mother country. Siphoning off many of Britain's most restless and ambitious souls, the United States provided a broader field of opportunity for those skilled in the use of the British technology. Returning from the former colony, English trade missions were frequently struck by the energy and extraordinary ingenuity of America's early manufacturers. Much like the Japanese in recent years, the Americans improved upon designs made in other lands and, in doing so, ultimately surpassed their teachers.

Like many of America's industrial giants during recent years, the British business elite failed to meet the challenge posed by upstarts from across the Atlantic. Losing their taste for the entrepreneurial struggle, they simply refused to modernize their factories, preferring instead to spend their fortunes on country manors and overseas investments. British investors helped finance many of America's early internal improvements, including the Erie Canal. By 1913, British industrial investment in the United States was equal to the equivalent in constant dollars of carrying out a Marshall Plan every two years. Fueled by this massive capital infusion, North America's share of world income between 1860 and 1913 rose from under 15 percent to nearly 33 percent; on the eve of World War I, America produced almost as much steel and coal, and more copper and electricity, as the whole of western Europe.[31]

On the Continent, where feudal ideas and institutions proved far less tractable, industrial progress occurred at a far slower clip. But by the late 19th century, France and Germany sought to catch up with Britain largely through state-directed initiatives. The Germans in particular sought to exploit economies of scale by encouraging huge industrial cartels similar to the great trusts in America. During the era of steel, automobiles, and chemicals, this strategy proved devastatingly effective. By 1897 Germany's giant-dominated economy achieved virtual parity with Great Britain; that year an English tract called *Made in Germany,* exploiting fears of decline, became an overnight best seller.[32]

In the aftermath of World War I, a new economic era dawned in Europe, one symbolized by Henry Ford's massive Detroit auto assembly plants. Charles Sable, in his brilliant *Work and Politics,* labels this new system "Fordism" for its reliance on mass production of standardized goods, routinized work rules, and giant corporate bureaucracies. Fordist ideas and images appealed to a remarkable range of European leaders, from Bolsheviks and Social Democrats to such industrialists as Giovanni Agnelli of Fiat and Louis Renault; when Czechoslovakia's first auto assembly line opened in 1925, the owners paid tribute to Fordism's homeland by naming the plant "America."[33]

But whereas Fordism in America, with its vast domestic markets and huge capital reserves, could develop under basically private auspices, in Europe the achievement of giant scale often required significant intervention and even ownership by the state. Not surprisingly, many prescient Europeans—among them Schumpeter, Sorokin, and Oswald Spengler—all saw the giant corporation as the precursor to some form of economic collectivism. As early as 1918 German industrialist Walter Rathenau commented:

> The depersonalization of ownership, the objectification of enterprise, the detachment of property from the possessor, lead to

a point where the enterprise becomes transformed into an institution which resembles the state in character.[34]

Since rising from the ashes of World War II, Germany and other European countries rebuilt their economies upon this conjunction of Fordist principles and state intervention. Eager to match America's dominant mass production industries, virtually every European nation sponsored their key industrial sectors, forcing the "rationalization" of smaller competitive firms or placing them under direct state control. With the election of a Labour government in 1945, even Britain, the home of Adam Smith, nationalized its hard-pressed coal, iron, and steel industries; French and Italian governments also maintained large interests in key industrial concerns in such fields as steel, telecommunications, and automobiles.[35]

But perhaps the most subtle form of giantism appeared in Germany, where the new Federal Republic developed a system of "organized state enterprise" in which giant industrial cartels, trade unions, and government officials worked together to promote industrial growth. Perfectly suited for large-scale, mass production industries, this strategy helped assure the return to primacy of such pre-war giants as Siemans and AEG-Telefunken. Led by its restored industrial giants, between 1950 and 1961 Germany experienced a remarkable "economic miracle" during which its per capita GNP doubled, a performance far superior to that of its major European neighbors. Although the system relegated small business and entrepreneurs to a minor role, this did not seriously affect German economic health until the dawn of the current technological era.[36]

Yet even as Europe's heavy industries were thriving, in part due to the infusion of some $100 billion in American capital,[37] the lack of entrepreneurial vistas prompted many of Europe's finest young minds to seek out better opportunities across the Atlantic. During the "brain drain" of the 1950s and 1960s, the Continent lost an estimated 100,000 scientists, engineers, and doctors to the United States. In the process Europe lost not only its technical resources, but a generation of high-tech leaders including Pierre Lamond, a future top executive with National Semiconductor; Dave Jackson, founder of Altos Computers; John Ellenby, future president of Grid Systems; and Wilf Corrigan, future chairman of Fairchild Semiconductor. Now chairman of LSI Logic, a semiconductor custom house in California's Silicon Valley, Corrigan blames the lack of opportunity for ambitious and innovative businessmen on the institutional conservatism of Europe's entrenched elite:

> Europe fell behind because technology wasn't the thing to do. You were supposed to be a doctor or a lawyer or banker. Only low-class people got involved in making things. The problem was at the top, in the nature of the societies. The governing elite in France was from the Sorbonne, in England from Oxbridge. Engineers had no status. They didn't rate.

With their native-born technologists deserting them, the governments of Europe sought out strategies to combat what Jean-Jacques Servan-Schreiber described as "The American Challenge." In the view of the influential French journalist and many others across the Continent, Europe's only hope lay in developing giant institutions capable of competing with American firms such as IBM and Boeing. Fixated on these giant-scale models, European technological strategy has been oriented toward creating large, government-backed firms, similar to those that helped the Continent regain its competitiveness in the basic industries.

With its long history of state planning, France led the way in developing this nexus of government and giant business. Under De Gaulle and his conservative successors, French government policy has been to "rationalize" major firms, particularly in such sensitive areas as computers, aerospace, and defense. "National Champion" firms were either started or melded together out of several smaller companies. These efforts produced a few successes, notably the French atomic energy program; others, among them the Concorde and the state-created computer firm, were notable disasters.[38] As one longtime French government official explained:

De Gaulle told us the nation needs big corporations. We encouraged mergers and acquisitions. Europeans were impressed with the IBMs, GMs, and Essos of America. The American invasion had telling results. We drew the conclusion that we needed giants. The same strategy we used in steel was applied to high tech; if there was no existent giant, we created one.

This belief in giantism continues to characterize French government under Socialist François Mitterrand. Borrowing heavily from abroad, the Socialists have promoted the centralization of French industry with a vengeance, boosting the government share of French industry from 18 percent to some 32 percent; among the largest firms swallowed up by the government have been two key electronics giants, Thomson and the Compagnie d'Électricité, giving the French government control of over 50 percent of their nation's electronics industry. Generous research funds have been lavished on these new government favorites which the socialists see as the key to making France the world's third major electronics power behind the United States and Japan. Boasts Mitterrand: "I am giving France its economic strike force."[39]

Other European nations have followed similar giant-scale approaches to high-technology development. Norway, Sweden, and Great Britain have all initiated massive government schemes to develop local electronics industries. Harvard's Robert Reich and other admirers of European methods have been particularly impressed with Germany's massive targeting of industrial research and development, totaling over $3.2 billion by 1979. For the last few years, elite bureaucrats at the German Ministry of Technology have lavished aid on firms trying to keep pace with American and Japanese advances in integrated circuits, semiconductors, and materials development.[40]

Yet in reality these attempts have not halted Germany's precipitous decline in the high-technology field. Once considered among the world's most sophisticated producers of electronic machinery, Germany's giant-oriented industrial strategy has failed miserably to provide the spark for high-technology growth. Indeed, in 1982 one of the nation's top electronics giants, AEG-Telefunken, collapsed under the burden of poor earnings and massive bank debts. Although AEG was the most noticeable failure, Germany's other semiconductor and computer industries also have continued to lag behind. Klaus Luft, vice-chairman of Germany's Nixdorf Computers, put it bluntly: "Basic innovation is lacking."[41]

Nor is Germany's failure an isolated case. After more than a decade of concerted effort, Europe remains hopelessly behind the United States and Japan in virtually every major new emerging industry, from computers and semiconductors to biotechnology. Between 1968 and 1980, the EEC's share of world exports in sophisticated products such as thermionic valves, electronic transistors, and circuitry dropped from 40.6 percent to a mere 27.2 percent, reflecting what the EEC staff itself called "a distinct deterioration" in Europe's competitive advantage. And by 1981, Europe's share of its *domestic* semiconductor market had plummeted to 40 percent, with the Americans holding the majority share. Admitted a 1982 EEC study: "Europe is no longer calling the tune. Europe is no longer in the van."[42]

The failure in high tech reflects an even more widespread decline in Europe's economy. Despite the claims of their American admirers, Europe's government-directed economies have failed to prevent the EEC nations from losing market share over the past decade in product categories from steel and cars to televisions and argicultural products. Spiraling government spending, used to prop up declining industries and to meet soaring social welfare costs, now totals over 40 percent of GNP in most European nations, far more than in either Japan or the United States. This mounting public burden, along with fast-rising wages, has cut deeply into the profitability of European business; during the 1970s the Continent's largest industrial corporations suffered net profits on capital less than half those enjoyed by American or Japanese firms. Not surprisingly, American investment in Europe has now slowed to a trickle.[43]

Only in Italy, where government interference has been largely blunted by its total incompetence, has there been anything close to an entrepreneurial renaissance. As the rest of Europe's economy has stagnated, Italy's has continued to grow; since 1978 it has boasted the Continent's largest gains in per capita GNP.[44]

Key to Italy's success has been the growth of its "hidden economy"—a network of small shops and factories accounting for as much as one-fifth of the national economy. Often started by workers laid off from giant firms, often too for reasons of political radicalism, Italian small companies have helped their nation remain competitive in such industries as high-fashion textiles, furniture, shoes, and leather goods. In towns such as Prato outside of Florence, over 15,000 small firms, mostly in garment-related trades and employing an average of less than five workers, have created a prosperous local economy with one of Europe's lowest rates of unemployment.[45]

The success of Italy's small firms has been bolstered by the government's inability or unwillingness to impose upon them the stringent tax and regulatory burdens borne by larger scale enterprises. Able to retain much of their capital, Italian entrepreneurs have developed a world-wide reputation for their ability to exploit new market niches quickly.[46]

Sometimes these small, family-oriented enterprises succeed on a scale of worldwide significance. Brescia, in the province of Lombardy, has long served as a center for small steelmaking enterprises. It was here that in 1914 Mario Danielli started his business of selling steelworking equipment. Moving to Buttrio, the firm expanded into the design of new equipment and eventually whole mills, including some 40 percent of the world's mini-mills, seven of them in the United States.

But Danielli's success actually has little to do with Europe. Most of the company's new projects are either in Third World countries, the Communist bloc, or the United States. Locked into their large, antiquated mills, European companies outside of Italy represented only 1 percent of Danielli's outstanding orders in 1982. Cecilia Danielli, granddaughter of the firm's founder and company president, sees Europe's reluctance to adopt the latest steelmaking techniques as symptomatic of a deepening Continental malaise. She points out:

> If Europe doesn't become a center of technical advance, there's no other solution. Ideas are our only real capital. But it's troubling. There's no real determination here.[47]

Perhaps nothing points up this lack of "determination" better than the Continent's failure to forge new job-creating industries. Dependent on larger established firms whose employment is dropping in Europe as elsewhere, the Continent produced only 2 million new jobs during the 1970s, compared to 5 million in Japan and over 19 million in the United States. Unemployment, once virtually nonexistent in the "organized state enterprise" economy of Germany, has reached double digit levels and could peak to 16 percent by the end of the decade, according to one government survey.[48]

As in the United States, deteriorating economic performance and growing trade deficits have led Europeans to look elsewhere for new economic paradigms. France's Mitterrand talks of turning his nation into the "Japan of the West," but the odds that socialists will be able to imitate the success of private sector-dominated Japan with its nationalizations are unlikely. Realizing this, critics of Mitterrand, including some within his own government, believe France's long-term economic future lies in creating the innovative, job-producing small firms like those now proliferating in the United States. Comments historian Fernand Braudel:

> If I were ruler [of France] I wouldn't worry about the larger firms, because to give them money is to prevent society from reforming itself. Instead of giving money to multinationals, I'd spend it on the smaller enterprises, because they're the ones that find the new solutions. A profound crisis requires a technological, structural renewal, and this rarely comes from the top. . . . The Industrial Revolution of the 18th century was pushed up mainly by very small enterprises.[49]

Recognizing the high-technology explosion in such areas as Boston's Route 128 and California's Silicon Valley, several European countries have attempted in recent years to promote their own entrepreneurial configuration. One European government, desperate for a way out of the technological cellar, even considered building a road around a major city in order to replicate Route 128's circuitous path around Boston.

Showing somewhat more perception, in 1976 France sent a team of top government and banking officials, headed by veteran civil servant Jean Deleage, to the U.S. to learn about California's venture capital industry. The French fund, Soffinova, did spectacularly well in the United States, helping launch such successful high-tech firms as Tandon Computers and Printronix.

But when Soffinova attempted to transfer its American lessons to France, the results proved highly disappointing. Timid state-owned and private financial institutions were reluctant to invest in fledgling high-technology firms; many family-owned companies, reflecting longstanding French tradition, steadfastly rejected the idea of selling off equity to outsiders. By 1979, Soffinova manager Jean Deleage had seen enough and late that year he quit in order to start his own venture partnership. Relaxing in his high-rise office overlooking San Francisco, the roundfaced, slightly rumpled Deleage explains: "After three or four years, I guess the entrepreneurial genius of America got to me."

In the face of this and other early setbacks, European governments are increasingly looking for ways to import "the entrepreneurial genius of America" to the Continent. Soffinova retains an active venture fund in America while both Britain and Germany have aggressively recruited such top U.S. venture capitalists as Jack Melchor and Peter Brooke to help launch venture funds in their countries.

But for these fledgling venture funds to succeed Europe must provide entrepreneurs with the opportunity not only to get started, but also to get rich. Perhaps the first important step in this direction has been the recent development in at least four European nations—

France, Sweden, West Germany, and the United Kingdom—of small issues-oriented markets. Based on America's over-the-counter exchange, these markets could give small firms a chance to raise the sort of equity now pouring into venture-backed firms in the United States. Divestitures and management buyouts, so important in the development of America's entrepreneurial configuration, are also sweeping into Europe; in 1981, one British firm alone expected to do over one hundred buyouts, ten times the number just three years previously.[50]

Yet despite these promising signs, Europe is far from an entrepreneur's paradise. High taxes and governmental tinkering tend to undermine the incentive of aspiring entrepreneurs, leading some to raise their funds in America or even move to the United States. For all the new rage about small enterprise development, Europe remains a continent dominated by the giantist ethos of the postwar epoch. As venture capitalist Peter Brooke sees it:

> There is a need for a whole revolution in how Europe approaches economic growth. The banks and governments in Europe traditionally have no interest in creating new, small businesses. They have substituted analyzing and planning problems for solving them.
>
> It's incredible that some Americans are going for heavy state planning when I'm being asked by Europe to help them disband theirs. We shouldn't follow their mistakes.

THE PACIFIC CHALLENGE

In 1945 Japan was a smoldering ruin, its industries devastated, its people near starvation. Foreigners occupying the nation spoke openly of returning it permanently to its preindustrial state so that it might never terrorize the world again.

Yet amid the charred remains of Tokyo, a brash young man charged around on a homemade motorized bicycle, hustling orders for his puttering contraption from the city's demoralized populace.

But although sales were brisk, few in the capital took Soichiro Honda seriously. A onetime Toyota subcontractor from rural Shizuoka, he was better known in the geisha houses than among the elite circle of Tokyo University graduates that had long dominated the nation's governmental and business scene.

But with many top *zaibatsu* ("money-cliques") chieftains implicated in Japan's wartime crimes, the nation's future now depended on self-starting entrepreneurs like Honda. With most Japanese wallowing in despair and apathy, only an eccentric like Honda would boldly scheme to put millions of his demoralized countrymen on his little motorbikes.

With capital raised from friends and his father, a backwoods blacksmith and bicycle repairman, Honda opened a small rural assembly plant in the late 1940s. Soon customers were coming from as far away as Kyushu, the southernmost of Japan's major islands, to buy the cheap, energy-efficient machines. Not satisfied with modest growth, the irrepressible Honda decided to expand his operation. In 1950, he opened a new factory in northern Tokyo. His request for supplies to build some three hundred motorcycles a month horrified officials at Japan's Ministry of International Trade and Industry (MITI). Honda's expansion plan, claimed one MITI official, "borders on insanity."[51]

But Honda was not to be dissuaded. Like many Japanese entrepreneurs of his generation, he was determined to expand his company despite all odds; among his contemporaries would rank many of the men responsible for creating the world's most envied economic success story, including such dynamic figures as Akio Morita and Masaru Ibuka of Sony, Konosuke Matsushita of Matsushita Electric, and Ryoichi Naito of Green Cross.

In a manner reminiscent of the early industrial entrepreneurs of Great Britain and America, Honda and his contemporaries built their success on a unique array of market instincts. Amid the most depressing conditions, these remarkable men believed fervently in themselves, their companies, and their nation. As Honda himself told the timid officials at MITI:

Even if my company becomes bankrupt because of the rate at which I expand my plant, the plant will remain to be used for the development of Japanese industry. So I will take the risk.[52]

Three decades later, Honda Motor Car sells over $7 billion in cars and motorbikes annually. Widely regarded as one of the world's best run manufacturing firms, it has consistently outperformed its most determined American, European, and Japanese competitors.

"Innovation," political scientist Michael Polanyi has written, "occurs on a crowded stage."[53] Honda arose amid a score of new and revitalized companies. These entrepreneurs, including some within the large Japanese firms, have developed a staggering array of significant new consumer products, such as Honda's stratified charge engine, Sony's Betamax, and Namco's Pac-Man. With an impact on industrial development as important as McCormick's reaper and Ford's assembly line, over the last three decades these innovations helped turn Japan into the capitalist world's second largest economy.

Yet most westerners ascribe Japan's success to virtually everything except the bold young outsiders who, perhaps more than any other force, provided the innovative spark for Japan's explosive growth. As Hiroshi Kato, a leading figure at MITI, has pointed out:

A risk-taker is an individual businessman no different from others in corporate growth style, behavior, and other factors, regardless if he is from the East or West. His presence is not peculiar to countries like the U.S. nor is it characteristic of the late 1960s and 1970s decade.

Any rational grown-up does have a dream of taking a risk once in his lifetime in the business he has chosen, which is a reflection of his romantic sentiment. This thinking is universally true of people beyond time and space.[54]

As Kato suggests, entrepreneurism is not an exclusively western invention; its effects have been felt in the shaping of capitalist economies around the world. Even before Japan's contact with the West, Japanese entrepreneurs were building an increasingly sophisticated array of commercial enterprises and even modest-scale factories making such products as sake and textiles.

As was true in contemporary Europe, businessmen in feudal Japan labored under a considerable social stigma; many of the earliest Japanese entrepreneurs came from either peasant stock or the ranks of petty samurai. Yet outsiders built much of the elaborate commercial infrastructure for Japan's future economic growth. As Father Maurice Bairy at Tokyo's Sophia University has suggested, Japanese society is like a wheel; the center remains highly conformist while those individuals spun off the fringes provide the essential innovative spark.[55]

Even the most established Japanese firms have their roots at the edge of Bairy's wheel. Mitsui Sokubei Takatoshi, founder of Japan's oldest trading company, came from a minor samurai family. In 1616 Mitsui decided to give up life "by the sword" and open a small sake shop. Mitsui's lack of business experience almost destroyed the enterprise in its first years of operation; only the intervention of his wife, Shuho, the daughter of a merchant, saved them from economic extinction. Within a century, due in part to her persistence and instruction of her sons, the family emerged as Japan's leading merchant house. By the time Commodore Perry forced open Japan to western trade in 1853, Mitsui had over 1,000 employees in its Tokyo operations alone.[56]

But the presence of American gunships in Tokyo Bay did much to quicken the pace of Japan's continuous revolution. By revealing the abject weakness of the ruling shogunate, Perry gave heart to rebellious provincial nobles, leading merchants, and samurai eager to overthrow the now decadent regime. Backed by merchant gold, rebels under the banner of the Meiji emperor Mutsuhito seized power in 1868.

To build Japan into a major industrial power, the new rulers needed to reform their society drastically. Although Japan's native industries produced excellent goods, the persistence of feudalism threatened to slow the pace of development. Fearful that westerners would soon overrun Japan with their advanced goods and weapons, the Meiji dynasty instigated a massive program of modernization. Government officials built the sinews of a modern industrial state—shipyards, cement factories, deepwater harbors, and spinning mills.

With feudalism's legal basis largely abolished, hundreds of thousands of the peasants who made up the majority of Japanese now swarmed into the cities and towns. Like Honda, some outsiders made it to the very top of Japanese business. Men from families of peasant background, the Iwasakis and Yasudas, formed the basis for two of Japan's great *zaibatsu* empires.[57]

Within the span of a few decades, these giant institutions, with their banks, numerous subsidiaries, and captive small contractors, achieved a status comparable to that of the trusts in America or the German cartels. Like their postwar descendants, the early entrepreneurial leaders of these firms feverishly acquired western technology and, aided by Japan's major banks, quickly established themselves in the world marketplace. Between 1900 and 1925, Japan's world trade increased almost tenfold; starting with such simple items as silk and yarn, Japanese industry moved toward higher value and added products like textiles, the bulk exported to neighboring Asian nations or the United States.[58]

By the mid-1930s the *zaibatsu*, according to an independent estimate made by *Fortune* magazine, controlled a remarkable 50 percent of the nation's financial assets and nearly three-quarters of Japanese business. The interests of these giant firms and national policy were so overlapping that some *zaibatsu* chieftains seemed to regard Japan's imperial conquests as adjuncts to their commercial strategy. "We have a splendid opportunity to expand abroad," exulted Fujihara Ginjiro, a leading Mitsui spokesman. "It is the manifest destiny of the Japanese nation."[59]

When the Americans occupied Japan in the fall of 1945, this collusion with the militarist "manifest destiny" prompted calls from Washington for the dismemberment of the *zaibatsu*. With the passion of Progressive era "trust busters," American officials laid out plans to split the great industrial combines into scores of smaller enterprises. They also preached the virtues of competition and independence to a whole generation of young Japanese, who increasingly looked to the Americans as role models. "The Americans," recalled economist Kazuo Kawai, "acted as the Japanese would have liked to act but could not because of their social inhibitions and thus the Americans became envied models of a desired conduct."[60]

In the process the American occupation helped to liberate Japanese business from the shackles of the class-conscious *zaibatsu* era. With many family hierarchs and their top minions banned from their old posts, a new generation of managers was provided an unprecedented opportunity to revitalize some of Japan's most important economic institutions. At Mitsui, for instance, Niizeki Yatsutari seized the reins of command at the firm's lowest ebb and provided the entrepreneurial spark leading to its full recovery. Others like Ishizaka Taizo took Tokyo Shibaura Electric (Toshiba) out of the Mitsui orbit, establishing it as an independent electronics giant of worldwide importance; Hitachi, once a satrapy of Nissan, also spun off to become a diversified manufacturer with its own cluster of subsidiaries. British historian G. C. Allen has observed: "The new freedom kindled many fires."[61]

Even many elements now associated with Japanese management had their origins in this era of openness and experimentation. Techniques of efficient steelmaking were first taught to Japan's infant industries by executives from United States Steel; many of the principles of quality control, including the "quality circles" now being rediscovered in America, had their origin in the postwar instruction of Japanese industrialists by such men as Walter Demming of General Motors. Japanese management, in essence, combined prewar practices like lifetime devotion to a single company with the most advanced American management techniques.

But it was foreign technologies that most excited the new Japanese entrepreneurs. Since the end of the war, Japanese firms have spent over $10 billion on the purchase of technologies from abroad, much of it American.[62] As the Japanese economist Terutomo Ozawa explains:

> In terms of the Schumpeterian paradigm, Japanese industry was engulfed en masse in a swarm of Japanese entrepreneurs who avidly acquired Western industrial arts. Since the technological gap was substantial, their effort to catch up extended over a prolonged period, resulting in continuous buoyancy of industrial activity accompanied by phenomenal growth in the stock of capital.[63]

Determined to maintain this "continuous buoyancy," Japanese government officials worked closely with the nation's leading banks and industrial companies to make sure funds were available for the capital expenditures of key growth sectors. Government policy targeted specific industries, regulated competition, and placed tough controls on foreign imports.

But despite this strong government role, it would be a mistake to confuse Japan's form of "controlled competition" with the centralized state planning common in European countries. Unlike the Continent, the government owned few of Japan's key industries; officials at agencies such as MITI worked instead through a combination of incentives and friendly persuasion. The government placed special emphasis on stimulating capital investment and savings; capital gains taxes were reduced to zero while other policies simultaneously encouraged growth, savings, and exports. Equally important, Japan's tax burdens were kept at a level lower than any major industrial nation. As William Rapp, a leading American expert on Japanese industrial policy, observes: "Japan predated the current 'incentive economics' by thirty years, and is living testimony of their validity."[64]

By the 1950s, moreover, MITI's once tight grip began to loosen. Mindful of the intense concentration in the American auto industry, MITI initially discouraged the formation of many of Japan's leading auto companies including Toyo, Honda, Mitsubishi, and Fuji, in order to preserve the international competitiveness of the two established auto giants, Toyota and Nissan. MITI officials even suggested the two largest car firms get together and manufacture a standardized "people's car." These proposals were fought and eventually defeated by Japan's automakers. Today, with eleven separate producers, Japan's automobile industry stands as the world's most competitive; since 1960 automobile production alone has risen from 474,000 to over 9.5 million annually. In 1980, automobile exports to the United States totaled over $8 billion, by far Japan's largest export item.[65]

As the auto industry example suggests, Japan's competitive ascendancy was not simply the product of brilliant government industrial planning. No one from MITI plotted Sony's move into radios; indeed, MITI resisted Sony's application for purchase of the American transistor patent so essential to its future success. Nor did the government design the strategy leading to superior Japanese innovation in a vast array of consumer electronics products from color televisions to the Betamax. Not even government research and development funds were responsible—Japanese government spending on R & D remains far lower than that of nations such as France and Germany and below that of the United States even when the Pentagon's enormous research budget is excluded.[66]

Yet today, the remarkable generation of entrepreneurs who spearheaded Japan's industrial ascendancy is now passing from the scene; without their inspirational leadership, some Japanese fear, their nation lacks the direction to continue its upward surge. According to polls of youth across the industrialized world, Japan's young people rank, as Frank Gibney has pointed out, "among the world's darkest pessimists." The sense of opportunity characterizing Japan's postwar continuous revolution is beginning to fade; the structures developed during the boom have taken on the rigid character of sprawling giant bureaucracies. As one Japanese executive told Honda biographer Sol Sanders: "The ice melted in Japanese society. But it has frozen over again."[67]

In many respects Japan, like America in the 1970s, is a victim of its own successes. Due to tremendous improvements in the standard of living, by the year 2020 Japan will have the highest percentage of people over 65 in the world. Already young Japanese commonly complain about the meager opportunities for promotion within the increasingly top-heavy giant firms. "I'm 35 and I have nowhere to go until I'm 50," complained one top Tokyo executive. "All my friends are running around like crazy but there's nowhere for them to go."[68]

These younger Japanese cannot be expected to work as dutifully as their predecessors. Between 1971 and 1980, the number of male university graduates wanting to change companies during their career more than doubled to almost 20 percent and those wanting to strike out on their own reached a remarkable one-third. Not surprisingly, the number saying that work was among life's pleasurable activities dropped nearly 50 percent during the decade.[69]

This weakening of traditional Japanese approaches to work comes just as many of Japan's most successful industries face an unprecedented challenge by newly industrialized competitors throughout the Pacific Basin. In recent years, Korea, Taiwan, Singapore, and Malaysia have all grown at rates faster than Japan and sometimes at Japan's expense. Intense competition from these nations and even from the People's Republic of China has undermined Japan's once powerful shipbuilding and textile industries. Perhaps most disturbing, these newly industrialized nations are following Japan's move into high technology. Electronics manufacturing job growth in South Korea and Taiwan has been expanding at four times the rate for Japan for the last two decades, a trend expected to accelerate in the future.[70]

Even steel, once the pride of Japan, now endures new competition, with steel imports from South Korea up some 47 percent in 1982. At the same time Japanese shipments to the United States declined to the lowest levels in fifteen years, reflecting stiffer competition from developing countries as well as American mini-mills. Raw material costs at twice those experienced by American firms have also decimated Japan's once soaring petrochemical industry. Imports, largely from the United States, have jumped from 24 percent in 1976 to 56 percent in 1981, according to estimates by the Hudson Institute.[71]

Unlike the United States, the depressed state of many Japanese industries is not the stuff of newspaper headlines. There is remarkably little bloodletting. Corporate executives with records of failure remain in place; government and private sector adjustment programs shift workers to other sectors of the economy. But although such steps are important for maintaining the fabled national consensus, they do not obviate the new economic realities bearing down on Asia's economic superpower. Even Japan's well publicized push into cutting edge high-technology industries is essentially a defensive move by a nation short of resources and pressed by increasingly vibrant competitors.

So far Japan's shift toward high technology has reaped some notable successes—for example, the lightning-quick takeover of the 64K Ram portion of the semiconductor market. But many leading Japanese realize that the 64K triumph may not be a harbinger of future trends, the conclusion so often drawn by American observers. As the pace of semiconductor technology quickens, the importance of creative engineering outweighs the traditional manufacturing strength of Japan's giant companies. Indeed, in such software-intensive products as 16 bit microprocessors, American firms outproduced their Japanese counterparts by better than 250 to 1.[72] Jiro Tokuyama, dean of the Nomura School of Advanced Management and a close advisor to Prime Minister Yasuhiro Nakasone, explains:

> Consensus is all right if you're trying to build an economy from scratch. Coordination is fine when you're building steel and cars on the model of other people. But now we are in the era of fast change, of integrated circuits and microprocessors. I don't think our large organizations can move quickly enough to make the changes.

Despite substantial, highly publicized government efforts to help Japanese firms develop their high-technology products in recent years, Tokuyama and other Japanese leaders believe America retains a formidable lead in most cutting-edge technologies. According to one MITI study, during the past two decades Japan's companies produced a mere 26 major technological innovations compared to America's 237; of those considered momentous by the scientific community, only 2 came from Japan, 65 from the United States. In 1979 America held a 7 to 1 technological trade balance over Japan in the crucial fields of electronics and communications.[73]

As Tokuyama and others have suggested, there is good reason to doubt that Japan's well-heeled, increasingly complacent corporations possess the innovative drive that so marked firms during the Honda era. In 1965, for instance, over 30 percent of all corporate R & D was devoted to basic research; by 1977 that figure dropped to less than 5 percent, with the bulk going to developmental research on technologies imported from abroad. Although Japan is now a net technology exporter, much of this comes from "recycling" existent techniques; by 1979 Japan's imports of new technologies from the United States were over three times its exports. A 1980 survey of technological development by the Japan Techno-Economic society found that 73 percent of the 200 top corporate managers believed that Japan still lagged behind the United States in revolutionary new technologies; nearly half said their firms failed to recognize the importance of creativity. As the respected monthly *Bungei Shuniu* put it:

> A feeling of crisis is spreading among Japan's technological experts. The closer engineers and researchers are to the factory floor and the more specialized they are, the fewer there are who think that Japan has forged ahead of the United States.[74]

Caught between aggressive Third World competitors and increasingly inflexible domestic corporate giants, many Japanese are once again looking toward models made in America. This time, however, they are not coming to Detroit assembly lines or inspecting the great blast furnaces of Pittsburgh. Instead they are traveling to precisely those places where high-technology entrepreneurship has been most marked; at a time when many Americans seem to think Japan has all the answers, increasing numbers of Japanese are trying to figure out the secrets of "the Silicon Valley Way."

In June 1982 one group representing the Osaka Junior Chamber of Commerce trekked to the Santa Clara Valley. After inspecting a large number of venture capital-backed technology firms, they came away convinced that the future belonged not to the giant-scale institutions of their homeland, but to the new breed of entrepreneurial firms spawned in the crucible of high-risk economics:

> The U.S. economy is faced with difficulties. . . . However, venture capital's innovations are effective in mitigating these symptoms of economic stagnation. There exists a system which enables people to apply large resources at high risk toward the commercialization of creative innovations. We should pay more attention to this system. [Japan's] problems cannot be solved solely by our large institutions. In order to cope with these problems without losing the vitality of a "free economic system," it is necessary for us to encourage high-risk entrepreneurship.

This growing interest in America's entrepreneurial configuration has even affected the elite bureaucrats at MITI. MITI now seeks to foster the creation of a dynamic small business sector in Japan. Central to the agency's new faith is the nature of the innovative technological businesses. Unlike autos or steel, high-technology industries don't necessarily improve with scale. As automated processing becomes more commonplace, a 1982 MITI report concluded, the "benefits of diversification . . . take the place of the benefits of scale in the various fields of business activity."[75]

Faced with this new paradigm, MITI has proposed some broad new initiatives to help the estimated 830,000 small manufacturing enterprises in Japan. Although these small and medium-sized firms contributed more to Japanese output than their American counterparts, the majority are subcontractors for larger companies and rarely expect to grow into larger, more independent enterprises. To break that cycle of dependence and spark their growth, MITI now is calling for the development of venture capital and other entrepreneurial finance mechanisms.

Although Japan's low interest rates remain the envy of many Americans, its rigid financial structure has made it difficult to support new entrepreneurial ventures. An attempt to start venture funds in the early 1970s floundered because of the conservatism of Japan's major commercial banks and the lack of a significant market for new issues. But today the Japanese government is not only seeking to encourage venture funds, but also to create a new over-the-counter market based on America's NASDAQ. Interest in entrepreneurial finance has also stimulated the movement of Japan's major banks to the United States; the purchase of the commercial finance subsidiary of Heller International and Mitsui's acquisition of Los Angeles-based Manufacturers' Bank, a highly successful small business lender, attest to Japan's interest in learning about American-style finance.[76]

But if Japan is to move successfully toward a more entrepreneurial economy, the key will lie with the younger generation of Japanese businesspeople. As Frank Kline, president of Pacific Technology Venture Management, a San Francisco-based venture firm specializing in the Pacific Basin, puts it:

There's a new generation in Japan. They are coming in with American ideas, even American educations. They don't want to join the traditional bureaucracies. They don't want the traditional subservient role of small business. They want to become entrepreneurs and they're looking for a way to do it. The coming of venture capital might make it possible. Japan is becoming uninhibited.

Kline's view might seem optimistic, but change surely is coming to Japan. Twenty years ago, Michio Sudo was destitute, riding the trains around Tokyo to keep warm on frigid days. In the distance, he saw the tall towers of the polluted Tokyo horizon and wondered how any man could create an empire large enough to construct such buildings. To most Japanese, Sudo's empire-building daydreams would have seemed patently absurd. The son of lower middle-class parents (his mother operated a little cake and ice cream shop in an unfashionable part of town), Sudo—like Soichiro Honda—was not part of Japan's tight-knit world of Tokyo University graduates, big company executives, and government bureaucrats.

In 1965, Sudo founded his Kangyo Denki Kiki Company in a one-room Tokyo office. His only employees were two women with a secretarial service who offered to answer his phones in exchange for the space. Working incessantly, he developed several new products, but no large firm would buy them. In 1973, he finally interested Asahi Chemical Company in a new car air bag; he traveled to Detroit to meet with GM officials, but was rebuffed once again.

That first trip to America and several that followed changed Sudo. In the United States, he saw entrepreneurs his age who had built new empires and high-rises to the sky. His determination redoubled, he continued to tinker. In 1980, with the help of two professors from Tokyo University of Technology, he invented a new "sheet coil" motor. Smaller and lighter than conventional small motors, this product appealed to Japanese consumer electronics companies, which make about 70 percent of the world's compact motors. With his sales approaching a $20 million annual rate, Sudo received a very American-style boost—a $250,000 investment from JAFCO, a new Japanese venture fund partnership. Relaxing for a brief moment in his hectic Tokyo offices, Sudo recalls:

It was in America that, for the first time, I started to think about the essence of things, how to think outside channels, without constraints. I went to places like California and saw how people interacted. I realized my dreams could be achieved. I was not only impressed with what I saw, I was inspired.

7

TWENTY-FIRST
CENTURY CAPITALISM

Amid the chaos of an uncertain present, a new capitalism is fighting
to be born. Although its origins are American, its influence can be
felt from the aging boulevards of Europe to the congested back-
streets of Tokyo. This new capitalism forged in the rapid technological changes of the past two decades, expresses itself in the increasing
demand by workers and managers for equity ownership, in the expanding multitude of small, successful innovative firms and in the
ascendancy of entrepreneurial finance over the steady routines of
conventional banking.

The new capitalism has reached a critical stage in the United
States because of its unique historical heritage. Alone among the
major nations of the world, America emerged full-blown into capitalism; the absence of a feudal epoch precluded the class stratifica-
tion of European and Japanese society. From the onset, the
American Revolution expressed a new individualistic ethos, one
shaped by the entrepreneurial aspirations of merchants, farmers,
and mechanics. The revolution placed America on the cutting edge
of history, inspiring other rebels across the Atlantic. "America," observes historian R. R. Palmer, "was the screen on which Europe
projected its own visions."[1]

Today America's entrepreneurial configuration provides a new model for a world increasingly dominated by collectivism. For a quarter century after World War II, the United States overwhelmed the world economy with its sheer industrial and agricultural might; now, in an era of greater international equality, its greatness can be assured only through the qualitative superiority of its technologies and business culture. As the French writer Jean-Jacques Servan-Schreiber has observed:

> I hope, indeed I believe, that one day America will wake up. . . . On that day, America will once again become not the dominant power—because that role is gone forever—but the exemplary power in the only competition that matters: the race to develop all men's abilities.
>
> On the day America awakes, it will give a decisive impetus to the rest of the world and contribute to the establishment of peace among men by the planetary advent of a society individualized by the new science.[2]

The future of this new "individualized" society, however, remains clouded in uncertainty—its ascendancy and its ultimate shape in doubt. Despite the powerful trend toward entrepreneurism, there also remain strong countervailing forces capable of eviscerating its progress. The very technology that has provided the gateway for a whole generation of entrepreneurs could, as they mature, play into the hands of cash-rich giant firms, including foreign companies with access to cheap capital. As automobiles and consumer electronics fell under the sway of giantism in the early 20th century abroad, so microelectronics and biotechnology could also fall victim to future waves of mergers and acquisitions. Ultimately, the fate of the American economy will hinge upon its people. How people *choose* to invest, manage their careers, and live their lives will prove more important to entrepreneurism's future and that of the country than any technological imperative.

A dynamic and entrepreneurial economy will require a commitment to industrialism. The rosy prophecies of today's trendy post-industrialists, with their blueprints of inevitable progress toward a technological and humanist millennium, are as dangerous as they are facile. The shortcut to heaven has been offered many times; every new technological advance, from the steam engine to electricity, has produced a crop of enthusiasts.[3] Yet problems continue to bedevil industrial societies through each technological era. As Joseph Schumpeter once observed: "We always plan too much and always think too little."[4]

This need to project a knowable future, so marked in these times, could undermine the opportunity to create even a livable present. The lure of a post-industrial millennium should not lead to celebration of the wrenching decline of the nation's basic industries. As widely acclaimed futurist John Naisbitt blithely states:

> . . . today, in fact, Japan is the world's leading industrial power. That is a little like a new-world champion in a declining sport, because the industrial companies of the world are getting out of those old industrial tasks.[5]

Naisbitt and other advocates of deindustrialization seriously underestimate the importance and basic strengths of America's manufacturing industries. Despite its marked ascendancy, Japan is not close to being the world's largest industrial power. In 1979, even before Japan's basic industries began suffering from the beginnings of obsolescence, American manufacturing output stood at better than twice that of the Pacific power.[6] In view of the even more overwhelming U.S. advantages in service and basic commodities, particularly food and coal, there is nothing inevitable about Japan's economic superiority.

But in the lives of nations ideas can do more damage than the works of competitors. In the last century, the elite of another nation with an economic empire as great as that of the United States also tired of the difficult and demanding tasks of industrialism. Great Britain in the mid-19th century was the world's industrial powerhouse. Its goods flooded the world, and its entrepreneurs created new markets and products with remarkable rapidity. But like some Americans today, the British capitalists disdained the muck of heavy industry and opted for the comfort and convenience of a purely service economy. "The rough and vulgar structure of English commerce," remarked Walter Bagehot, ". . . the sweet essence of its life was snuffed out."[7]

In such an atmosphere, even the most determined industrialists soon lost heart. They stopped modernizing their plants and equipment. And workers, without confidence in their bosses, accelerated the trend by resisting innovation. Over the generations, the sons of the rough-hewn capitalists of the Industrial Revolution became the professionals, the bureaucrats, the international financiers of the world. They lived splendidly insulated from a domestic economy sliding toward permanent obsolescence. Even before the outward symptoms of the "British disease" became evident, there had already occurred, as historian Martin Weiner has pointed out, "a psychological and intellectual deindustrialization."[8]

THE SEMICONDUCTOR SHOWDOWN

Over the past decades, the United States has displayed many of the early symptoms of the "British disease." The giants of steel and electronics have meekly surrendered the technological initiative to more aggressive competitors overseas, creating economic havoc for the Midwest and other regions. But as many established companies lost the industrial spirit, America's continuous revolution has ushered in a new generation of entrepreneurs committed to the future of a manufacturing and goods-producing economy.

Perhaps nowhere is this faith more profound than in the semiconductor industry, the emerging bastion of the American economy. In the words of Advanced Micro-Devices founder Jerry Sanders, semiconductors are "the crude oil of the eighties." The analogy is an apt one. Just as oil-based energy provided the foundation for the explosion of the chemical industry and other heavy industries during the postwar era, semiconductors provide the essential building block for modern microelectronics. According to an Arthur B. Little report, this industry will expand to $500 billion by 1988, and by 1990 will actually be larger than either automobiles or steel. Equally crucial, semiconductor products constitute an increasingly pivotal element in a broad range of industries; application of this technology will soon determine the health of virtually every key economic sector. As a 1980 Worldwatch paper puts it:

Many of the industries that have been leading employers such as those producing automobiles, chemicals, appliances, and so on, are likely to incorporate microprocessors and small computers into production processes to improve productivity. Microprocessors make possible new automation technologies, like computer-controlled welding machines, or, for example, the microprocessor-controlled machine that screws light bulbs into the instrument panels of GM cars.[9]

The centrality of the semiconductor industry to virtually every sector of the American economy should disprove the trendy notions of "sunrise" or "sunset" industries so pervasive today. Without a healthy semiconductor industry, it is unlikely that the basic industries in the United States will be competitive. And without basic industrial customers—the largest consumers of integrated circuits— the future of the American semiconductor companies will be equally bleak.[10]

From its early days the semiconductor industry expressed the full dynamism and innovative power of America's entrepreneurial configuration. Although based on work done at Bell Laboratories and subsidized by military contracts, entrepreneurial companies sparked the commercial application and phenomenal growth of the semiconductor industry. In 1958 it was two emerging medium-sized companies, Fairchild and Texas Instruments, that developed the semiconductor into its commercially usable progeny, the integrated circuit (IC).

Sparked by this new technology, between 1966 and 1972 thirty new semiconductor firms entered the market, including some twenty-one out of Fairchild alone. Usually founded by dropouts from larger firms, companies such as Intel, National Semiconductor, Advanced Micro-Devices, Mostek, and Analog Devices created a competitive environment unparalleled throughout the world. An exhaustive study by UC Berkeley's Roundtable on the International Economy observed that these firms:

> [reflected] a shining example of two venerated features of competitive capitalism: the success of venture capital-backed entrepreneurship, and the triumph of the innovativeness of the small firm. . . . it is competition across this structure that has produced technological progress and market diffusion in the United States and sustained the international competitiveness of the U.S. electronics industry as a whole.[11]

This emerging entrepreneurial configuration—with its procession of strong established companies, market-driven medium-sized firms, and aggressive, small start-ups—gave the United States unquestioned command of world semiconductor markets. By 1975 American firms controlled 98 percent of the domestic IC market, 78 percent in Europe, and nearly 20 percent in Japan, despite trade barriers.[12]

But by the late 1970s, the Japanese emerged as major competitors on a worldwide scale. Taking advantage of a severe shortage of venture funds brought about by the 1974–75 recession and high capital gains rates, Japanese firms such as NEC aggressively moved into production of new standardized products (among them, 64K RAM chips), capturing the lion's share of the world market and over half of the American domestic consumption by the early 1980s.[13]

Much of this Japanese upsurge has been widely credited to MITI's decision to "target" semiconductors as part of a national strategy to achieve "international superiority" for its industries.[14] But perhaps more crucial have been the long-range strategies of Japan's leading electronics giants. Flush with profits from their earlier triumphs and boosted by an almost inexhaustible supply of capital costing well below that of their American competitors, Japanese firms such as Hitachi, NEC, and Toshiba invested heavily in the latest semiconductor manufacturing processes, using their captive domestic markets to provide the necessary volume. As is traditional in Japanese business, these firms accepted low profit margins and quickly captured the large markets in such standardized products as 16K and 64K RAM chips. Seth Godwin, industry analyst at Paine Webber in New York, explains:

> Japan's international competitive strength is not the result of lower wages, high productivity, automation, government R & D spending, or interest rates. It is instead the result of the fundamental differences in the structures of the Japanese and U.S. economies.[15]

Japan's capture of these key semiconductor markets shocked many American businessmen and politicians. Even such respected industry figures as Don Valentine, L. J. Sevin, and Ben Rosen feared the U.S. microelectronics industry had met its Waterloo. In Japan, self-satisfied officials at the nation's giant electronics firms stripped away the mask of deference and declared their contempt for the entrepreneur-driven American industry. Speaking of such firms as Advanced Micro-Devices, Intel, and National Semiconductor, Atsuyoshi Ouchi, senior vice-president of Nippon Electric, declared in 1980:

> Boutique-style integrated circuit producers have no place in the highly competitive marketplace, whether their plants are in Silicon Valley, Silicon Island [Kyushu], or anywhere else where they are produced. Too many U.S. producers are too small.[16]

Yet today these "boutique" producers have mounted a massive counterattack on the Japanese monolith. Unlike the giants of consumer electronics, the entrepreneurial leaders of American semiconductor firms have no intention of meekly surrendering their markets. Responding to the Japanese challenge, Intel company officials launched a "125 percent solution," expanding the work week to fifty hours for most of its employees. At Advanced Micro-Devices longer working hours were also imposed, while at National Semiconductor a program called "quest for quality enhancement strategy" inspired greater productivity in its manufacturing operations."[17] Boosted by these and other steps, U.S. semiconductor makers increased production by $275 million and captured nearly 70 percent of the world market, even in the face of recessionary conditions. And in 1983, the newly deregulated Western Electric Company announced it would produce the next generation of computer chips, the 256K Ram, well ahead of its Japanese competitors.[18]

But perhaps the greatest threat to Japan's goal of worldwide semiconductor supremacy lies in the fast-changing nature of the technology itself. Advances in the manufacture of customized semiconductors and integrated circuits have created a whole new field for entrepreneurial ventures. Since 1980 over twenty-three firms have entered the semiconductor market,[19] most concentrating on either advanced custom circuits or totally new semiconductor technologies. In this new era of "new dynamic instability," as Michael Borrus describes it, America's entrepreneurial configuration has definite advantages over the more structured Japanese firms. Even such hard-boiled industry veterans as Don Valentine and L. J. Sevin, who as late as 1980 had sworn off semiconductors, have now re-emerged as lead investors in these new start-ups. As Valentine explains:

Something has changed very dramatically. There are new areas to get into. We're getting a real change in structure. The Japanese were good in mass-producing 16 or 64K Rams but that's only part of the story. Everything else is crap. Their PR is better than their output. Semiconductors simply have proven not to be a classic mass production industry. The pace of change is quickening and that doesn't lend itself to what they're good at.

The two to one American lead in the fast-growing custom chip market could be a crucial step in maintaining the nation's industrial world supremacy. Recognizing this, some of the top industrial firms have helped finance the equipment purchases of new innovative "silicon foundries" and other semiconductor start-ups. At the same time, forward-looking giants such as IBM have teamed up with Intel, Rolm, and other emerging firms to further the American advance in the new technologies. This increased private sector cooperation, not a protectionism or the imposition of foreign models, provides the best hope, not only for semiconductors, but also for American industry in general. As long as America's entrepreneurs provide "a moving target" by constantly innovating, observes Berkeley's Borrus, they will become far less susceptible to "targeting" by such agencies as MITI.[20] Warren Davis, director of governmental affairs for the Cupertino, California-based Semiconductor Industry Association, points out:

We don't have to meet MITI with MITI here. The way for everyone to win is through interdependence, not through creating a Fortress America. The people running our semiconductor companies are still entrepreneurs. They need to be free to fail.[21]

A BUSINESS PLAN FOR AMERICA

To give entrepreneurs the freedom to fail, they must believe they have a chance to succeed. In the increasingly brutal international marketplace, American firms often find themselves competing against companies with far cheaper sources of capital, import restrictions, and other governmental subsidies. A free marketplace has done much to make the United States the world's leading technological power. The challenge is to preserve that marketplace without undermining the American players within it.

American growth companies such as those in the semiconductor field neither need nor, for the most part, desire government subsidies or protection. Attempts to "protect" crucial industries like semiconductors can only lead to increasing rounds of protectionism and, ultimately, to the decay of the current world economic system. Nor should policies adopted in Japan or France be taken as models for the United States. Comments Berkeley's John Zysman:

> U.S. policy will not succeed by attempting to imitate directly a system different from our own. We cannot and would not want to transform our system into theirs, and we wouldn't run that system as well as they do. We must make our own system work more effectively.[22]

As Zysman suggests, America's industrial strategy must be shaped, through the capital markets, to its fundamental strength—the innovative power of our entrepreneurial companies. Centralization of investment or subsidization programs in Washington would inevitably play into the hands of entrenched interests that have long dominated the political process. Few entrepreneurs believe Washington possesses the wisdom to target specific companies or make investment decisions. "I guarantee you that no government official can target the right industry; in fact, I'll almost guarantee they'll target the wrong ones," observes Nolan Bushnell, the peripatetic California entrepreneur who founded Atari and Pizza Time Theater. "The targeting role belongs to entrepreneurs."

Perhaps the most pressing problem facing those entrepreneurs is the cost of capital. Unlike their foreign competitors, American entrepreneurs in semiconductors and other capital-intense industries often do not enjoy access to cheap sources of credit. Moreover, Japanese firms can leverage their debt-to-equity by a ratio of as much as 10 to 1, almost ten times more than American firms.[23] U.S. companies, beset by higher interest rates and more dependent on the fickle equities market, face a real cost of capital three times that of their Japanese competitors, according to a study prepared for the

American Business Conference by George Hatsopoulous of Thermo-Electron Corporation.

This differential has had devastating impact on a whole range of American industries. But perhaps the worst effects have been felt by small and medium-size growth companies in the high-technology sectors. To compete with their foreign adversaries, these firms must consistently upgrade their facilities and commit a large proportion of their available funds to research and development. As Hatsopoulous observes:

> We are being crippled by the cost of capital—that is the central issue. If the Japanese can get theirs so cheap, we will all be noncompetitive in everything, including high tech. If we don't change things, the entrepreneurial firms will die or be acquired. It could be catastrophic.

To prevent high capital costs from extinguishing America's entrepreneurial companies, the nation's tax and financial systems must be reformed dramatically. Reducing large federal deficits and assigning a more realistic value to the dollar in relation to other currencies, Hatsopoulous suggests, would be a good start. A more immediately realizable step, however, would be granting cumulative preferred stock dividends—the return to equity investors—the same tax-deductible status now accorded to interest payments. That simple step alone, according to Hatsopoulous, could reduce Japan's capital cost advantage on a $10,000 product from $2,300 to only $700.[24]

Not only must the *cost* of capital be brought down, but there should be adequate incentives for it to flow into the productive segments of the economy. In 1978 the nation's largest companies sat atop some $80 billion in ready cash, but instead of spending it on plants and equipment, much went to finance acquisitions or pay dividends.[25] A deft and productive instrument in the hands of entrepreneurs, capital is frequently less so when left at the disposal of conglomerate managers.

To shift capital toward the entrepreneur will require a major rehauling of the nation's banking system. Deregulation has so far concentrated on the liability side of the balance sheet. New money market certificates netted giant banks such as Chase Manhattan over $50 billion in December 1983, but the reform did little to encourage large banks to lend more to entrepreneurial firms. Sweeping revisions of regulatory procedures, now favorable to large-scale loans, should be implemented to reduce the bias against lending to small and medium-size firms. For example, the wide difference in leverage requirements between large banks and smaller ones, traditionally the source of long-term loans to small businesses, should also be lessened in order to assure a more "level playing field" for financial institutions. Steps should be taken to encourage the banking system to provide long-term loans to small companies. As Iowa's Congressman Jim Leach observes:

> We have, through government rules and regulations, given incentives to invest abroad through lending abroad. That lending policy is something that has skewed economic growth [away from the U.S.] . . . If small banks keep having greater restraint on their growth, then the dollars in the areas they serve, such as small business, are less than the dollars that go into other societies.

This same prejudice against lending to entrepreneurs has been particularly marked among pension fund managers. With over $800 billion in their coffers, pension funds represent the single most important source of capital in the nation—constituting almost two-thirds of all new capital flowing into financial markets.[26] Yet for years legal precedents (for example, the "prudent man rule") mandated only the most conservative investment vehicles, such as "blue chip" stocks and bonds, for pension investments. Recently, the spectacular results enjoyed by funds investing in venture capital have begun to change this tradition of conservatism. An intelligent reform of pension fund investments, observes leading expert Lawrence Litvack, could do much to correct "inefficiencies in capital allocation" developed during the long years of giant-oriented regulation.[27]

The nation's tax code, as well, must be weaned from its pro-giant bias. Tax laws favoring large corporations with powerful lobbies as reflected in the 1981 "safe harbor leasing" law and accelerated depreciation have allowed giants such as General Electric to pay negligible taxes. In contrast, medium-size growth companies, including the members of the American Business Conference, consistently pay twice the effective tax rate of the nation's 100 largest firms.

Instead of rewarding failure, an entrepreneur-oriented tax system would incentivize innovation, risk, and success. The spectacular results from the capital gains reduction of 1978 suggest the power of such "incentive economics." Since the 1978 reduction, over $5.5 billion in new venture investments have been made, largely in young high-technology companies. These firms have produced so much in new employment, goods, and services that capital gains reduction has actually boosted revenues to the Treasury.[28] VLI founder Bruce Vorhauer remarks:

... Entrepreneurs shouldn't have a free lunch. Adversity breeds strength. What we need to do is create a climate that encourages entrepreneurs. Cutting the capital gains gives everyone the incentive to try his own crazy scheme. The government has to think about our motivations, not about what can help the bureaucrats at Exxon. The entrepreneur should not be so grossly undervalued.

To accelerate the growth of firms like VLI, the capital gains taxes on investments directly into the treasuries of companies should ultimately be reduced to zero, if the investment is for at least three years. In addition, a change allowing small firms to retain the first $500,000 in profits without paying corporate taxes would greatly enhance the ability of entrepreneurial companies to grow in the crucial years before they have access to public equity and private venture capital markets.

Similarly, there should be further boosts in investment and research and development tax credits. This is particularly critical for firms in the semiconductor and other advanced technological fields, and would greatly help small companies such as those in semiconductor technology that normally spend up to 15 percent of their revenues on R & D, five times the average for manufacturing firms. Other incentives should be provided for investments in manufacturing equipment.[29] As Michael Borrus has observed:

> The new competitive strategies of U.S. semiconductor producers will help them succeed in the market only if U.S. firms can successfully make greater capital investments in R & D and new manufacturing systems. . . . The Japanese are in part counting on the semiconductor industry's increasingly heavy capital burden to eliminate the dynamic competitiveness of the merchant sector of the U.S. industry.[30]

Small-firm R & D could be further boosted by allowing them to write off the salaries of creative personnel, who often account for the largest percentage of their R & D expenditures. Similarly, research funds spent on software development, a key to success for many small high-tech firms, should not be denied tax credits as the IRS proposed in 1983. Such a move, observes M. S. Forbes, would constitute "a tax on knowledge"[31] at a time when software expertise constitutes a critical factor in American high-technology competitiveness.

But no systematic tax reform plan should supply aid to firms only in the semiconductor or computer fields. Increasingly, the health of America's economy will depend to some degree on the ability of small firms to purchase productive equipment. Steps should be taken to reward those entrepreneurs who are willing to spend on new systems. An investment tax credit for purchases of used capital equipment over the current minimum of $100,000 would help these small companies upgrade their plants and productivity. Along with high-technology firms, small manufacturing companies have been the prime generators of new manufacturing employment.[32] Mel Boldt, owner of a suburban Chicago machine shop and president of the Independent Businessmen's Association of Illinois, asserts:

The laws have always been passed so that the big guys have the advantage. But in the future there will be needs for smaller volumes, more precise work. That's what we do, but we need the incentive to get the right equipment.... It's not like we're looking for a handout. We're offering the solution.

Despite a growing awareness of the importance of these small and medium-sized businesses, implementing an economic strategy that supports the entrepreneurial process will probably take years of intense political struggle. Attempts to reform the tax system, with the exception of the 1978 capital gains reduction, have so far been stymied by entrenched economic forces.

For instance, Los Angeles accountant Harvey Goldstein has been trying to persuade Congress to pass the Small Business Investment Incentive Act for over two years. Designed to provide tax incentives for investors in America's fifteen million small firms, it would allow small businesses to raise as much as $250,000, with investors receiving up to $15,000 in immediate tax deductions. The measure would help bring capital to a whole realm of service and manufacturing proprietors who cannot hope to borrow long-term from the banks or reap investments from venture capitalists or the public marketplace.

This act, according to such sponsors as the National Federation of Independent Business, would bring $1 billion to small firms and help create over 100,000 new jobs. The total cost to the Treasury would be no more than $50 to $100 million. But to the Washington political establishment, which spends billions on the most misconceived notions, this modest proposal aiding entrepreneurs seems the height of lavishness. Despite some twenty congressional sponsors, Goldstein's bill is likely to remain bottled up until the small business community gains the power to push it through. As Goldstein, a

member of President Reagan's National Productivity Advisory
Committee, points out:

> This part of the economy deserves more than mere lip service.
> We as a nation spend millions on welfare, millions for arma-
> ment, and only a few dollars to assist this most vital segment of
> our country. . . . It's been in vogue to say that people support
> small business. There's been a lot of verbiage. Now we're going
> to start to put the challenge to them.[33]

THE POLITICAL PROSPECT

Propelled by their economic successes, entrepreneurs must now be
ready to mount that political challenge. No longer willing to remain
the odd men out in national politics, entrepreneurs are organizing
themselves into an independent, coherent political force. To accom-
plish this, however, they will have to overcome the very individualistic—even egocentric—impulse central to their own character. Says
John Rennie, chairman of Massachusetts-based Pacer Systems Corporation and president of the 1,500-member Smaller Business Association of New England:

> The nature of these folks is very diverse. We have our high-
> techers and low-techers, extreme liberals and extreme conser-
> vatives. You look at them and say, "Damn, how do you build a
> political constituency out of such a motley group?

Stymied by their own diversity, entrepreneurs have traditionally
been outlobbied by the more cogent interests of the giant institutions, with their legions of lobbyists and lawyers permanently
planted in the nation's capital. But since the 1978 capital gains reduction, there has been a steady upsurge of political activity among
small and medium-sized companies. After the 1980 White House
Conference on Small Business, entrepreneur-oriented groups—
including Small Business United, the National Federation of Inde-

pendent Business, the American Business Conference, and the American Electronics Association—began to present a significant counterweight to the entrenched "bigs" of business, government, and labor. According to American Business Conference Chairman Arthur Levitt, "We have spawned the most powerful lobby in the economic history of the nation."[34]

Levitt's claim may seem a trifle extreme today, but perhaps not so for the future. Since the New England merchants and artisans launched the American Revolution, emerging economic groups have ushered forth new political movements including the Jeffersonian Republicans, the Democrats of the Jackson, Bryan, and Wilson eras, and the Progressive followers of Robert La Follette and Hiram Johnson.

Today the bearers of this tradition come not from the forests or the plains, but from the frontiers of new technologies and ways of thinking. The technological businessmen in California's Silicon Valley or Boston's Route 128 have only recently begun to challenge the giants' stranglehold on national political power. As Sandra Kurtzig, chairperson of ASK Computers, admits: "Politics has usually been the last thing on my mind."

But since the 1978 capital gains triumph, Kurtzig and other high-tech entrepreneurs have taken an increasingly active political role. In 1979, for instance, Massachusetts's burgeoning high-technology community, distressed at the ill effects of that state's extremely high taxes, played a central role in the passage of tax-cutting measure Proposition 2½. Similarly, on a national level most entrepreneurs supported Ronald Reagan and other conservatives who were willing to pledge lower taxes. Many later became disenchanted when the 1982 recession boosted bankruptcies to a post-Depression high and left the entrepreneurial constituencies up for grabs.

Increasingly, entrepreneurs are beginning to move beyond their narrow antitax position. Faced with increasingly strong competition from abroad, they are beginning to look at government not as an implacable foe, but a potential ally. Intel chairman Robert Noyce told the *San Jose Mercury*'s John Hubner:

Five years ago politicians were anathema. The industry took a "leave us alone and let us do the job, don't bother us and we won't bother you" attitude.

Today we are being severely challenged by other national governments that have recognized the importance of the high-tech industry. For us to stay in competition, some government action has to be taken.[35]

Noyce and other entrepreneurs agree broadly on what they seek from government. Most believe that maintenance of the basic infrastructure—roads, bridges, schools—constitutes an essential precondition for industrial progress. Similarly, as the nation adapts to new technological imperatives, there will be an increased need for new job skills. Local government agencies, like community colleges, should be adequately funded to provide the personnel they need. Close link-ups between local entrepreneurial communities and school districts—such as the "High-Tech High School" set up with industry assistance in Silicon Valley—should be expanded to train people for jobs that exist.

But the role of government need not be circumscribed by only the most immediate current needs. Just as government created the pre-market conditions necessary for the settlement of the West, tomorrow the space program could help create new horizons for entrepreneurs, laying out the highways to the stars. Already the space program has given birth to new technologies in weather prediction, pollution control, lubricants, and protective coating.[36] Indeed, one 1975 study by Chase Econometrics projected that NASA R & D would by 1984 add over $83 billion to the GNP, a better than 8 to 1 return. Like the pioneers who followed the path of the cavalry to the West, a whole new generation of entrepreneurs is emerging to move into space industries, a probable $20 billion industry by the year 2000. As astronaut Robert Crippen puts it: "American ingenuity shows that if there's a buck to be made, somebody will make it."[37]

Yet if American ingenuity is to prevail, in space or elsewhere, there must be new political leadership. Even as leaders in both major parties turn their gaze to the entrepreneur as the nation's best hope for economic revival, it has become painfully clear to entrepreneurs that the Washington establishment understands little about who they are and what they need. Nothing better illustrates this fact than the increasing calls by top political leaders for strict protectionist measures for autos and other threatened industries, including high technology. And nothing could be more contemptuous of the fundamental competitive principles that drive most entrepreneurs. Continental Steel's Tom Sigler explains:

> Protectionism is not the answer to our long-run problems in this industry. Meeting the competition, getting the elements together to meet it, that's what made this country. . . . If we can't get ourselves ready to meet the challenge, we're the fools and deserve to lose. And I hate to lose.

Perhaps even more infuriating to entrepreneurs are the attempts to use the nation's economic problems as an excuse to impose top-down government planning. Whether to bail out "sunset" industries such as steel or "sunrise" high-tech firms, the placing of broad investment powers in the hands of politicians or an elite corps of government bureaucrats has little support among entrepreneurs.

This opposition is based not only on their low opinion of government's abilities to make investment decisions, but also on the fear that large firms will dominate any targeting process. The aggressiveness of top big business leaders such as Felix Rohatyn of Lazard Frères, John Galvin of Motorola, Howard Love of National Steel, Charles Brown of AT&T, and Irving Shapiro, former DuPont and Business Roundtable chairman, in pushing such proposals has done little to reduce this suspicion.[38] Silicon Valley venture capitalist John Friedenrich says:

> If you have targeting, the Motorolas are going to get their share, but the small guys can't be so sure. Big companies have a proven ability to extract what they want from the political pro-

cess. You could have targeting in the name of technology and kill the spirit that's getting the things done.

To ensure policies that target "the spirit" and not the balance sheets of the giants, entrepreneurs themselves must get involved in the political process. Politicians may praise entrepreneurs for the jobs and wealth they create, but when the time comes to vote, the big contributors from large corporations and labor unions usually carry more weight. In 1982, for instance, the American Electronics Association contributed $24,000 and the National Federation of Independent Business $267,000 to political campaigns; compared to the $2.4 million of the American Medical Association or the $400,-000 war chest of Standard Oil of California, entrepreneurial political action committees amount to insignificant nubbins.[39]

Although small business and entrepreneurs will probably have to boost their care and feeding of politicians, a more direct approach might also prove effective. Increasingly, entrepreneurs are taking active part in the process themselves as the best way to insure their input in key political decisions. In states such as Tennessee and Massachusetts well organized small business groups have established a powerful political presence.

But in the end, this new constituency will need leaders who understand their needs instinctively. In this regard, the election of such entrepreneurs as New Jersey Senator Frank Lautenberg, Senator Lloyd Bentsen of Texas, and California Congressman Ed Zschau could stand as harbingers of a new and important trend. Richard Silberman, former California state budget director and longtime entrepreneur in such diverse industries as fast foods, banking, and electronics, observes:

I don't think either party's political establishment has the program for the entrepreneur. The reality is that neither has the intellectual equipment to deal with the problems in industries such as high tech. The politicians are just going to zigzag until entrepreneurs themselves get in there and do it.

THE EXISTENTIAL CHALLENGE

The resurgence of the entrepreneur on the stage of world history marks a crucial moment in the history of capitalism. By reintroducing the human factor into economic life, the entrepreneur may save capitalism from over a century of giantism and ever greater depersonalization.

It is the fate of capitalism to either become entrepreneurial or ultimately lose the cause for its existence. As early as 1848 Karl Marx observed that by the logic of ruthless accumulation, capitalism would develop into a scale that undermined its own individualistic basis. If concentrated in a few hands, Marx noted, capitalism would become "like a sorcerer who is no longer able to control the powers of the nether world who he has called up by his spells."[40]

In Marx's view, the capitalist entrepreneur stood at the heart of economic progress but inevitably would be doomed by ever larger units of capital. For Marx and his followers, this "cash nexus" would inevitably lead to crisis in capitalism and usher in a new socialist millennium. Despite the presence of such grotesque progeny as the Soviet Union, this vision of capitalism and its decline remains a powerful force for hundreds of millions of human beings.

But it was the decidedly non-Marxist Joseph Schumpeter, writing nearly a century later, who saw in the emergence of the giant corporation the ultimate agent of capitalism's downfall:

> The perfectly bureaucratized giant industrial unit not only ousts the small or medium-sized firm and "expropriates" its owners, but in the end also ousts the entrepreneur and expropriates the bourgeoisie as a class, which in the process stands to lose not only income but also what is critically more important, its function. The true pacemakers of socialism were not the intellectuals or agitators who preached it but the Vanderbilts, Carnegies, and Rockefellers.[41]

Despite these prognostications, America, virtually alone among the world's largest countries, has escaped the socialist purgatory assigned to it by the wisest of seers. In the face of ever increasing corporate giantism and even against the threat of mammoth government and labor bureaucracies, the entrepreneur has stood against history and survived. By doing so, he has not only enriched economic life, but preserved the capitalist system for all its myriad players. "The strength of capitalism," remarked Lenin, "lies in the strength of its small business enterprise, but small business still survives in a large degree in America, giving birth to the middle classes, constantly, hourly, spontaneously and on a mass scale."[42]

To survive, capitalism must appeal to more than a mere handful of well-heeled individuals. The recent entrepreneurial ascendancy has its roots in a broad-based desire throughout society for great economic and personal self-determination. It owes much to the great individualist rebellions of the 1960s—ranging from the Goldwater movement on the right to the student New Left. Both movements sought to break the tutelage of the large, bureaucratic institutions that dominated American economic and political life. As declared in the 1962 Port Huron Statement, one of the earliest statements of the Students for a Democratic Society:

> We regard *men* as infinitely precious and possessed of unfulfilled capacities for reason, freedom, and love. In affirming these principles we are aware of countering perhaps the dominant conception of man in the twentieth century: that he is a thing to be manipulated, and that he is inherently incapable of directing his own affairs.[43]

Two decades ago, this quest for individual self-determination among the idealistic young led to political action, then radicalism, and, sadly, to increasingly totalitarian ways of thinking. But those values enunciated at Port Huron have seeped into society and become part of its mainstream. As Daniel Yankelovich has observed, the new "cultural revolution" is based on opposition to "instrumentalism," the use of people as tools of production and distribution.[44]

In this epoch, entrepreneurism cannot survive as an isolated phenomenon involving only individuals. The revulsion against control is not only relevant for the entrepreneurial elite; it exists within men and women throughout the occupational spectrum. By 1977, 54 percent of all Americans claimed the *right* to take part in decisions affecting their jobs; among younger workers, nearly two-thirds expressed this sentiment.[45]

Cognizant of this desire, many corporations now try to accommodate the yearning for self-determination among their workers. Even such giants as Chrysler, U.S. Steel, General Mills, Honeywell, and General Electric have begun programs to incorporate greater worker participation. Comments Cambridge, Massachusetts-based management consultant Barry Stein:

> There's a real shift of attitude among companies. It isn't even arguable anymore. There's a recognition that how you organize your people can make the main difference. You can't take them for granted. And you can't just throw money at the problem. There's no way to capitalize your way out of the problem of human beings.

Large companies, however, have only limited options for employing "the human factor," Stein asserts. Size and bureaucracy are the natural enemies of self-determination, even for managers. Equally important, large firms, with their already enormous and diverse blocks of owners, have far less flexibility to take self-determination to its logical next step, worker ownership.

More than any single factor, the future of capitalism rests on replacing its current "cash nexus" with a new equity nexus. Worker-owned firms and cooperatives have existed in America since the 1790s, but only recently has the "equity nexus" become an important feature on the American landscape.[46] In 1976, 300 American firms offered some form of employee ownership plan; in 1979, the number had swelled to 3,700; today it stands at over 5,000.[47] In 500 of these, the workers own a majority of the stock.[48]

The increasing popularity of worker ownership has much to do with the enviable record of success in such companies. Although the degree of control exercised by workers varies sharply, the results in terms of productivity and profitability have been nothing short of spectacular. A University of Michigan study, for instance, found that firms with some worker ownership enjoyed profits 1.5 times those of conventional firms; another report, prepared by the University of Iowa in 1980, found that companies with Employee Stock Option Plans (ESOPs) enjoyed a 78 percent increase in productivity in contrast to a 74 percent drop among their non-ESOP counterparts.[49]

Combined with humanistic management, worker ownership can create an atmosphere tailor-made for growth. At Materials Research Corporation in Orangeburg, New York, President Sheldon Weinig credits his package of job security, free educational opportunities, and stock options for MRC's employee turnover rate averaging 20 percent below that of other manufacturing companies. Weinig, whose company boasts annual sales over $71 million, explains bluntly, "If people have no long-range interest, you'll do nothing but create bad employees. You have to have a common cultural climate. I'm working to get people to bust their ass for me but they'll only do that if we are in touch with their needs. We can't make money hating each other."

Perhaps nowhere has this equity nexus been more important than in the entrepreneurial growth companies in high technology. At companies such as Intel, for instance, employee incentive is heavily weighted toward stock options; a similar approach exists at virtually every major high-technology firm. The incentives can be tremendous, particularly in small start-up firms. When Tanden Computers went public in 1981, nearly ten employees became millionaires while even assembly line workers reaped stock benefits up into the $100,000 range. "Widespread ownership of stock options," observes Silicon Valley venture capitalist Reid Dennis, "has been a tremendous contributor to the growth of these companies. It's one of the greatest socialistic devices in the world. It's *the way* to spread the wealth."

Although not as common in other sectors, worker ownership schemes can be found in scores of industries. Among the more successful firms with broad worker ownership are People Express, a New Jersey–based airline, the Record Factory, a San Francisco area record store chain, the *Milwaukee Journal,* and JANCO, a Los Angeles aerospace firm.[50] New legislation, both on the state and federal levels, can be expected to expand use of ESOPs and other worker ownership devices in the coming years.

But perhaps worker ownership's greatest promise may be in the supposedly "dying" basic industries. In 1980, General Motors decided to close down its Clark, New Jersey roller bearing plant. For GM, the unionized plant had become a nightmare of antiquated machinery and excessive featherbedding. Desperate, the automaker sold the factory to its employees, who boosted productivity 50 percent and put the firm back in the black within a year.[51] Similar stories have occurred in plants scattered across the industrial belt from Lewiston, Maine to Waterloo, Iowa. All told, worker ownership has helped save an estimated 50,000 industrial jobs from extinction.[52]

The success of worker ownership has even impressed union officials, who traditionally view stock options as a device to weaken employee solidarity. Some prominent union leaders, such as Communications Workers of America president Glen Watts, believe worker ownership and unionism are compatible. At Kokomo's Continental Steel, steelworker local president Bill Collins negotiated shares of up to one-third of the company's equity as part of a wide-ranging package to save the ailing company. "This is really our company now," Collins asserts. "We all have to get into the entrepreneur thing."

But for the entrepreneurial ethos to succeed, it must ultimately pervade not only the union hall or the tinkerer's garage, but also the minds of the new generation of managers. For decades, however, the nation's leading business schools have inculcated a managerial mentality totally oriented to the needs of large, bureaucratic corporations. The curricula for MBA students at such elite schools as

Harvard and the University of Chicago reflect this corporatist bias; a 1977 analysis of the standard Harvard MBA casebook found only one percent of the best-selling cases pertained to small business.[53]

This bias against entrepreneurial companies has characterized many graduates of the best business schools. The "new managerialism" of the early 1970s—stressing the primacy of cash management over particular product lines—was in large part a product of the Boston Consulting Group, an offshoot of the Harvard Business School.[54] Jack Steele, a graduate of Harvard and for seventeen years a professor at Stanford's Business School, recalls:

> We stopped teaching leadership at the schools. We helped create a generation of CEOs who were nothing but glorified bureaucrats. They cared about procedures, how to do the technical stuff. We created managers who wanted to do things right, instead of leaders who would do the right things.

Today, however, as dean of the University of Southern California's School of Business, Steele believes "there's a revolt among MBAs against the Fortune 500." In 1968, only seven business schools offered entrepreneurial courses; today over 150 of the nation's over 1,000 MBA programs have either full-scale entrepreneurial programs or several courses dealing with small business-related subjects.[55] At Stanford University, the nation's top-ranked business school, located in the intellectual heart of the Silicon Valley, nearly a quarter of graduating MBAs opted for jobs in firms with under 100 employees.[56]

This shift from big business reflects the growing attraction of the emerging entrepreneurial configuration for the young. Even at Harvard, where the average graduate can make in excess of $40,000 a year by entering an investment banking or consulting firm, a 1982 survey showed some 37 percent were interested in entering a small firm upon graduation and nearly 85 percent hoped eventually to work within a small company during their career. The school's Small Business Club, once insignificant, now includes nearly one-third of the MBA class. As club vice-president Howard Glass explains:

The 1980s are different. The entrepreneur is now the hero around here—Steve Jobs on the cover of *Time* and all that. In the 1960s everyone wanted to be a consultant. In the 1970s it was investment banking. Now it's who's going to start the next Apple.

In this new environment even the giants are changing. Once confident in their hierarchical splendor, the nation's leading companies are now trying to somehow transform their sprawling organizations with the elixir of entrepreneurship. In place of the money management of the Boston Consulting Group, corporate leaders today yearn to create the sort of drive, intimacy, and imagination characteristic of the burgeoning smaller firms.

For years giants such as Xerox, 3M, and Texas Instruments pioneered the internalization of entrepreneurship by setting up small, limited product groups. More recently IBM, deeply concerned about its huge but diminishing percentage of the computer market, developed Independent Business Units (IBUs) to foster more independent decision-making. The fourteen IBUs established since 1981 function as "companies within a company" and have already achieved broad success, particularly with the IBM Personal Computer, which booked sales of over $500 million in less than a year and a half.[57] Yet despite the success of the IBUs, the giants are unlikely to achieve the efficiency and dynamism of smaller firms. In the early 1970s more than thirty of the nation's hundred largest firms started venture capital projects, most of them oriented to creating new fields of corporate diversification. Most failed within five years.[58] Despite sometime heroic efforts, the attempts by large firms to diversify through internal venturing have not been spectacular successes. As a Harvard Business Review study of internal corporate venturing concluded:

Still, questions about the innovative abilities of large companies persist. Their incentive structures poorly suit entrepreneurial individuals willing to stake savings and careers on new ventures, and their organizational hierarchies make difficult the identification and rewarding of true innovators.[59]

In the face of this experience, some giants are resorting to the old formula of acquiring innovation and markets by buying entrepreneurial firms. Gould, for instance, has made such an acquisition strategy the centerpiece of its high-technology strategy. But the history of acquisitions, particularly in high technology, has been one of repeated failure; few of the semiconductor firms bought by larger companies in the last decade, including Fairchild and Mostek, have achieved anything like the success of entrepreneur-led firms such as Intel, Advanced Micro-Devices, or National Semiconductor.

In the future, it may well be that the larger firms will do better by investing in the entrepreneurial companies. In 1982 IBM made huge investments in two highly innovative firms, Rolm and Intel, without attempting to take control. Similarly, Acme-Cleveland Corporation, a major machine tool maker, has started investing in small firms in order to achieve a "window" on new technologies. Like IBM, Acme could have swallowed its tiny investment targets but wisely chose not to. Company President Roy C. Kuhn explains: "These are brilliant, independent individuals we could more than likely never employ."[60]

Perhaps Kuhn's comment signals an awakening in the consciousness of America's giant corporations. For decades, these firms relentlessly searched the economic horizon for companies and ideas. Believers in their own destiny, they tried to dominate the American economy through the "cash nexus," and without knowing it, fulfill the collectivist prophecies of Karl Marx and Joseph Schumpeter. Nevertheless, the entrepreneur has survived and come back with a daring and spirit not seen since the early days of the Industrial Revolution.

Behind this change is the one element missing in the equations of prophets and managers alike—the human factor. In 1980, Barry

Dickman was a bright young computer scientist from Georgia. His fledgling company, Image Automation, was just getting off the ground when he received an offer that seemed almost too good to be true. Exxon, the nation's largest company, wanted to buy Image Automation and offered Dickman a high-ranking position in its multimillion-dollar Exxon Enterprises venture unit.

Dickman was flattered. The newspapers and magazines were full of talk about Exxon's push into the office information business. Suddenly, at 30, he found himself in plush offices, surrounded by secretaries and subordinates, directing R & D at a $100 million unit of the billion-dollar giant.

But soon he was having second thoughts. Although active in such exploding new technologies as word processing, Exxon Enterprises couldn't seem to get the hang of the high-technology marketplace. In 1980 alone the company Information Systems group lost a staggering $150 million on sales of only $270 million.[61] "I thought I'd be impressed by these sophisticated corporate guys," Dickman remembers. "What I found out was that these very sharp guys from RCA or Sperry couldn't move fast in a new venture. They could manage an installed base, but they didn't have the spirit to create one."

Finally fed up with corporate torpor, Dickman quit in July 1981. He had never failed before and was determined to prove himself again. So in early 1982 he started another company, Noetics, with the modest goal of taking on such companies like DEC in the minicomputer market. His money running out, still searching for venture funding, Dickman feels no regret for leaving the secure womb at Exxon for the uncertainty of the entrepreneurial struggle:

Exxon was good to me—maybe too good. They provided all the money in the world. They promoted me. I was on the super-fast track. But I think back and wonder what it all meant. There I was, just a mark out on their multibillion balance sheet. Now I've got worries, but I'm building something—bringing something new into the world or at least taking the risk to try it. I think in the big company you're just too insulated. There's no existential challenge.

NOTES

1. THE HUMAN FACTOR

1. Thomas Cochran, *American Business in the Twentieth Century* (Cambridge, Mass.: Harvard University Press, 1972), p. 184; Kirkpatrick Sale, *Human Scale* (New York: Coward, McCann & Geoghegan, 1980), p. 25.
2. George Lodge, *The New American Ideology* (New York: Alfred A. Knopf, 1975), pp. 111, 165.
3. Statistical Abstract of the United States, U.S. Department of Commerce, Washington, DC, 1981, p. 390.
4. David Birch, *The Job Creation Process*, MIT, March 1978; David Birch, "Who Creates Jobs?" in *The Public Interest*, Fall 1981, p. 3; Job Creation, Hearings before the House Small Business Committee, p. 3.
5. *Fortune*, annual listing of 500 largest industrials, May 2, 1983.
6. Sale, *Human Scale*, p. 310; David Birch, Corporate Evolution; analysis of county business patterns by size, 1965 through 1980, conducted by David Pardo (based on U.S. Census data).
7. Frederick Jackson Turner, *The Frontier in American History* (New York: Holt, Rinehart, 1920), p. 154.
8. George Gilder, *Wealth and Poverty* (New York: Basic Books, 1981), p. 63.

9. Edward S. Greenberg, *Serving the Few* (New York: John Wiley, 1974), p. 244.
10. Joseph Schumpeter, *Capitalism, Socialism and Democracy* (New York: Harper & Row, 1947), p. 131.
11. Pitirim Sorokin, *The Crisis of Our Age* (New York: E. P. Dutton, 1941), pp. 185–86.
12. Cochran, *American Business in the Twentieth Century*, p. 86.
13. *Ibid.*, p. 75.
14. FTC Report, "Effects of Conglomerate Mergers" (Washington: Government Printing Office, 1972), pp. 12–14.
15. Daniel Bell, *The Coming of Post-Industrial Society* (New York: Basic Books, 1973), p. 79; John Kenneth Galbraith, *American Capitalism* (Boston: Houghton Mifflin, 1952), p. 91.
16. Gerhard Mensch, *Stalemate in Technology* (Cambridge, Mass.: Ballinger, 1979), pp. 183–84.
17. D. C. Mueller, "Conglomerate Mergers," *Journal of Banking and Finance,* December 1977, pp. 320–21.
18. Sidney Lens, "Reindustrialization: Panacea or Threat?" *The Progressive,* November 1980, pp. 44–47.
19. *State of Small Business,* U.S. Small Business Administration (Washington, DC: Government Printing Office, 1983), p. 41; Linda Grant, "Superpay: Justified or Out of Line?" *Los Angeles Times,* August 19, 1982; Tom Redburn, "Harvester: Breadth of Operations Diluted Energies," *Los Angeles Times,* August 8, 1972; Linda Grant, "Executive Pay Often Outstrips Performance," *Los Angeles Times,* August 22, 1982; Carol Loomis, "The Madness of Executive Compensation," *Fortune,* July 12, 1982.
20. "The New Lean, Mean Xerox," *Business Week,* October 12, 1982.
21. Ernest W. Walker, ed., *The Dynamic Small Firm* (Austin: University of Texas, 1975), p. 3; "Employee Ownership: Issues, Resources and Legislation" (Arlington, Virginia: National Center for Employee Ownership, 1982), p. 2.
22. This was the result of an extensive review of SIC Code 357 (Of-

fice Machines and Computing Equipment) for the Department of Commerce through 1965–80, broken down by size; material collated and analyzed by David Pardo, PhD candidate in finance, University of Southern California.
23. Norman Macrae, "Intrapreneurial Now," *The Economist,* April 17, 1982.
24. Modesto Maidique, "Entrepreneurs, Champions and Technological Innovation," *Sloan Management Review,* MIT, Winter 1980, pp. 59–73.
25. *National Science Foundation Science Indicators,* 1976, National Science Foundation, Washington, DC; Gelman Research Associates, *The Relationship Between Industrial Concentration, Firm Size, and Technological Innovation,* Report for the Small Business Administration, Office of Economic Research, Office of Advocacy, May 11, 1982.
26. "IBM: The Colossus That Works," *Time,* July 11, 1983; F. M. Scherer, *Industrial Market Structure and Economic Performance* (Chicago: Rand McNally, 1970), pp. 361–62.
27. Office of Technology Assessment, "Technology and Steel Industry Competitiveness" (Washington, DC: Government Printing Office, June 1980), p. 3.
28. Mark R. Reinganum, "Abnormal Returns in Small Firm Portfolios," *Financial Analyst's Journal,* March–April, 1981.
29. All the steel and computer companies included were listed on the New York or American Stock Exchanges during the period between 1963 and 1981. Steel and computer firms were divided into ten groups according to capitalization values, ranked from smallest to largest. Average returns were computed for each group, not adjusting for risk. The companies were then grouped into three categories—small, medium, and large. Weighted average returns were then computed for each group (David Pardo).
30. Tracy Herrick, "Small Banks: A Growth Industry," private study, Palo Alto, California, 1983.
31. "The New Entrepreneurs," *Business Week,* April 18, 1983.

32. Durwood L. Alkire, "Small Business Tax Problems," excerpted from Hearings Before the Subcommittee on Access to Equity Capital and Business Opportunities, Committee on Small Business, House of Representatives (Washington, DC: Government Printing Office, 1980), pp. 183–99.
33. Memorandum, Kent Hall staff economist to Parren Mitchell, Chairman, House Committee on Small Business, October 14, 1982, and conversations with Steve Coll, Community Information Project.

2. THE ENTREPRENEUR AND THE ESTABLISHMENT

1. Fernand Braudel, *Capitalism and Material Life, 1400–1800* (New York: Harper & Row, 1973), p. 320.
2. *Ibid.,* p. 108; Louis M. Hacker, *The Course of American Economic Growth and Development* (New York: John Wiley, 1970), pp. 111–13.
3. Turner, *The Frontier in American History,* pp. 93–94.
4. Thomas Paine, *Common Sense* (Woodbury, NY: Barron's Educational Services, 1975), p. 81.
5. Stuart W. Bruchey, ed., *Small Business in American Life* (New York: Columbia University Press, 1980), pp. 66–71.
6. John C. Miller, *The Federalist Era* (New York: Harper & Row, 1960), p. 32.
7. Charles Beard, *An Economic Interpretation of the Constitution of the United States* (New York: Free Press, 1965), p. 25.
8. Alexis de Tocqueville, *Democracy in America,* Volume One (New York: Vintage Books, 1944), p. 53.
9. Henry Nash Smith, *Virgin Land* (Cambridge, Mass.: Harvard University Press, 1970), p. 154.
10. Jonathan Hughes, *Industrialization and Economic History* (New York: McGraw–Hill, 1970), pp. 131–37.
11. Hacker, *The Course of American Economic Growth and Development,* p. 248.

12. David E. Koskoff, *The Mellons* (New York: Thomas Crowell, 1951); Stewart H. Holbrook, *The Age of the Moguls* (Garden City, NY: Doubleday, 1953), p. 61.

13. Thomas Cochran and William Miller, *The Age of Enterprise* (New York: Harper & Row, 1968), pp. 121–28.

14. Richard Hofstadter, *The Age of Reform* (New York: Alfred A. Knopf, 1955), pp. 64–65.

15. Spencer C. Olin, *California's Prodigal Sons* (Berkeley: University of California, 1968), pp. 90, 177.

16. Hacker, *The Course of American Economic Growth and Development*, pp. 257, 269–70; Hofstadter, *The Age of Reform*, p. 251; Gabriel Kolko, *The Triumph of Conservatism* (Chicago: Quadrangle Press, 1977), pp. 90–254.

17. John Tipple, *The Crisis of the American Dream* (New York: Pegasus, 1968), p. 21.

18. Cochran and Miller, *The Age of Enterprise*, p. 304.

19. Daniel R. Fusfeld, *The Economic Thought of Franklin Roosevelt and the Origins of the New Deal* (New York: Columbia University Press, 1956), p. 213.

20. *Ibid.*, pp. 38–57, 100.

21. Seymour E. Harris, *Saving American Capitalism* (New York: Alfred A. Knopf, 1948), p. 202.

22. Kim McQuaid, *Big Business and Presidential Power* (New York: Morrow, 1982), p. 94.

23. *Ibid.*, pp. 74, 84–85; Theodore K. Quinn, *Giant Business: Threat to Democracy* (New York: Exposition Press, 1954).

24. Otis L. Graham, Jr., *Toward a Planned Society* (New York: Oxford University Press, 1977), p. 48.

25. *Ibid.*, p. 49; "The Question of Abolishing the Reconstruction Finance Corporation: Pro and Con," Washington, DC: *Congressional Digest*, April 1953.

26. Francis X. Sutton, Seymour E. Harris, Karl Kaysen, and James Tobin, *The American Business Creed* (New York: Schocken, 1956), p. 21; David E. Lilienthal, *Big Business: A New Era* (New York: Harper, 1952), pp. 7, 33.

27. John Bunzel, *The American Small Businessman* (New York: Alfred A. Knopf, 1962), pp. 76, 80, 257–58.

28. McQuaid, *Big Business and Presidential Power*, pp. 123–24; C. Wright Mills, *The Power Elite* (New York: Oxford University Press, 1956), p. 285.

29. McQuaid, *Big Business and Presidential Power*, pp. 199–219.

30. *Ibid.*, p. 220; John Kenneth Galbraith, *The New Industrial State* (Boston: Houghton Mifflin, 1971), p. 58.

31. Richard J. Barber, *The American Corporation* (New York: E. P. Dutton, 1970), pp. 13–14.

32. Leonard Silk and Mark Silk, *The American Establishment* (New York: Basic Books, 1980), p. 292.

33. *Ibid.*, p. 254; Barry M. Hager, "Business Roundtable: New Lobbying Force," *Congressional Quarterly*, September 17, 1977, pp. 1964–68; Martin Tolchin, "Carter's Corporate Brain Trust," *New York Times*, July 24, 1978.

34. Robert Wolcott Johnson, "The Passage of the Investment Incentive Act of 1978: A Case Study of Business Influencing Public Policy" (unpublished PhD thesis, Harvard University Graduate School of Business), p. 131 ff.

3. MAKING IT AS AN OUTSIDER

1. "1983's Fastest Growing Small Public Companies," *Inc.*, May 1983; United California Bank, "Recent Economic Trends and Indicators," 1980.

2. Henry Nash Smith, *Virgin Land* (Cambridge, Mass.: Harvard University Press, 1970), p. 247.

3. Carey McWilliams, *California: The Great Exception* (Santa Barbara: Peregrine Smith, 1976), p. 66.

4. Richard H. Peterson, *The Bonanza Kings* (Lincoln: University of Nebraska Press, 1977), pp. 10–12.

5. Carroll W. Pursell, ed., *Readings in Technology and American Life* (New York: Oxford University Press, 1969), pp. 150–56.

6. Gene Bylinsky, *The Innovation Millionaires* (New York: Scribners, 1976), p. 78.

7. Kirkpatrick Sale, *Power Shift* (New York: Random House, 1975), pp. 31–32.

8. "Litton Industries' Charles 'Tex' Thornton," *The Executive,* January 1980, "A Rejuvenated Litton is Off Again to the Races," *Fortune,* October 8, 1979.

9. Robert Wolcott Johnson, "The Passage of the Investment Incentive Act of 1978: A Case Study of Business Influencing Public Policy" (unpublished PhD thesis, Harvard University Graduate School of Business), p. 88.

10. "Location of High Technology Firms and Regional Economic Development," report of Joint Economic Committee, U.S. Congress (Washington, DC: Government Printing Office, 1982).

11. Peter J. Brennan, "Advanced High Technology Center Santa Clara, California," report issued in 1980 in conjunction with Development Counselors International, Inc.

12. Lenny Siegel, "Delicate Bonds: The Global Semiconductor Industry," Pacific Studies Center, Mountain View, California, January 1981.

13. Don C. Hoefler, "Captains Outrageous," *San Jose Mercury Sunday Magazine,* June 28, 1981.

14. "Regional Patterns of Venture Capital Investment, 1981," Department of Commerce, Small Business Administration, p. 14.

15. Siegel, "Delicate Bonds: The Global Semiconductor Industry."

16. "United Technologies and Mostek: After the Acquisition," *Mergers and Acquisitions,* Spring 1982.

17. "The One Hundred Fastest Growing Small Public Companies," *Inc.,* May 1983.

18. "Regional Patterns of Venture Capital Investment," p. 14.

19. L. Rodriguez, *Dynamics of Growth* (Austin, Texas: Madrona Press, 1978), pp. 52–53; Thomas Cochran, *American Business in the Twentieth Century* (Cambridge, Mass.: Harvard University Press, 1972), p. 198; population statistics from Chase Econometrics study quoted in *New York Times,* January 10, 1982.

20. Stanley H. Brown, *Ling* (New York: Bantam, 1972), pp. 41–50, 244–84.
21. *Texas Fact Book,* 1980, Bureau of Business Research, University of Texas, Austin, 1980, pp. 2–3.
22. Brown, *Ling,* p. 34.
23. John McDonald, "The Men Who Made T.I.," *Fortune,* May 1961.
24. *Ibid.*
25. James M. Howell, "Risk Taking, Technological Innovation and the Future of the Northeast" (draft of speech courtesy First National Bank of Boston, 1983).
26. Nancy S. Dorfman, "Massachusetts High Technology Boom: An Investigation of Its Dimensions, Causes and the Role of New Firms," Center for Policy Alternatives at the Massachusetts Institute of Technology, April 1982.
27. Russell B. Adams, *The Boston Money Tree* (New York: Thomas Crowell, 1977), p. 9.
28. Carroll W. Pursell, ed., *Technology in America: A History of Individuals and Ideas* (Cambridge, Mass.: MIT Press, 1981), p. 10.
29. Adams, *The Boston Money Tree,* p. 33.
30. *Ibid.,* pp. 36–37.
31. Arthur Mann, *Yankee Reformers in the Urban Age* (New York: Harper & Row, 1954), p. 12.
32. *Ibid.,* pp. 187, 267.
33. Adams, *The Boston Money Tree,* p. 267.
34. Gene Bylinsky, *The Innovation Millionaires,* pp. 81–82.
35. Thermo-Electron, Annual Report 1982; Teradyne, Annual Report 1982; Millipore, Annual Report 1982.
36. Bylinsky, *The Innovation Millionaires,* pp. 82–83.
37. *Ibid.,* pp. 82–85.
38. "Regional Patterns of Venture Capital Investment," p. 14; and "Location of High Technology Firms and Regional Economic Development," pp. 9–13.
39. Dorfman, "Massachusetts High Technology Boom," p. 105.

40. "American Survey: New England," *The Economist,* May 9, 1981.

4. HEROES OF THE HEARTLAND

1. *Auto Community Adjustment Plan,* Report to the Secretary of Commerce, Community Planning and Development, March 1981, p. 3; "Kokomo has experienced economic sunshine, storms," *Kokomo Tribune,* October 19, 1975.
2. From selected historical data, City of Kokomo.
3. *A Sketch of the History and Growth of the Continental Steel Corporation* (Kokomo, Indiana: Continental Steel, 1952).
4. Gene Bylinsky, *The Innovation Millionaires* (New York: Scribners, 1976), p. 55.
5. "America's Restructured Economy," *Business Week,* June 1, 1981; and Frank Cassell, "Manpower Changes 1982–2000 Chicago–Midwest," October 15, 1982 (unpublished paper, Northwestern University).
6. David L. Birch, speech to Symposium on Small Business, Council of North Central Governors, Green Bay, Wisconsin, March 4, 1982.
7. *State of Small Business, 1983,* Small Business Administration, p. 43; "The New Face of Manufacturing," *Venture,* October 1982.
8. Lindley H. Clark, "Service Revolution: Too Much Too Soon," *Wall Street Journal,* April 13, 1982; *C& ID Reports,* Illinois Department of Commerce, Vol. 1, issue 3, 1983; and A. James Heins, "The Illinois Economy: An Analysis of Growth in Illinois 1948 to Present" (paper prepared for Illinois Chamber of Commerce), 1983.
9. "Parts of the city have become economic wastelands," *Chicago Tribune,* May 12, 1981.
10. Frederick Jackson Turner, *The Frontier in American History* (New York: Holt, Rinehart, 1920), pp. 151–53.
11. *Ibid.,* pp. 155–56, 205.

12. Bessie Louise Pierce, *A History of Chicago: 1848–1871,* Volume 2 (New York: Alfred A. Knopf, 1957), pp. 6, 103–7; Carroll W. Pursell, ed., *Technology in America,* pp. 71–79.

13. Dan J. Forrestal, *Faith, Hope and $5000* (New York: Simon and Schuster, 1977), pp. 14–39.

14. Louis M. Hacker, *The Course of American Economic Growth and Development* (New York: John Wiley, 1970), p. 248.

15. Annual Rankings of Largest Industrials, *Fortune,* May 2, 1983.

16. Jonathan Hughes, *The Vital Few* (New York: Oxford University Press, 1973), pp. 283–95.

17. *Ibid.,* pp. 289, 294; Walter Adams, ed., *The Structure of American Industry,* fourth edition (New York: Macmillan, 1971), pp. 71, 258.

18. Alfred P. Sloan, Jr., *My Years with General Motors* (Garden City, NY: Doubleday, 1972), pp. 3–43.

19. Hughes, *The Vital Few,* pp. 283–95; Pursell, *Technology in America,* pp. 174–75.

20. Sloan, *My Years with General Motors,* p. 4.

21. Statistics from staff report, Bureau of Economics, Federal Trade Commission (Washington, DC: Government Printing Office, 1963).

22. *Conglomerate Mergers—Their Effects on Small Business and Local Communities,* Report of the Committee on Small Business, House of Representatives (Washington, DC: Government Printing Office, 1980), pp. 13–14.

23. J. D. Glover, *The Attack on Big Business* (Cambridge, Massachusetts: Harvard University Press, 1954), p. 169.

24. Phillip I. Blumberg, *The Megacorporation in American Society* (Englewood Cliffs, New Jersey: Prentice–Hall, 1975), pp. 74–78.

25. Mark Green and Robert K. Massie, Jr., eds., *The Big Business Reader* (New York: Pilgrim Press, 1980), p. 490.

26. Charles Tavel, *The Third Industrial Age* (Oxford, UK: Pergamon Press, 1980), p. 194.

27. Louis Fleming, "Plant Closings Profitability Edging Out Social

Costs," *Los Angeles Times,* January 1, 1983; "Rust Bowl: Jobs Fade as Steel Mills Waste Away," *Los Angeles Times,* April 25, 1983.

28. "Location of High Technology Firms and Regional Economic Development," Joint Economic Committee, Congress of the United States (Washington, DC: Government Printing Office, 1982), p. 9.

29. State of Illinois brochure, "Move Your Company to Illinois: The State of the Art," 1982; "Regional Pattern of 1981 Venture Capital Investment," *Venture Economics* report for the U.S. Small Business Administration, December 1982.

30. "A Black Cloud Over the Smokestack Industries," *Business Week,* October 18, 1982; "Industry Report," Oppenheimer and Company, November 12, 1982.

31. Joseph Wyman, "The Steel Industry: Quarterly Commentary," Joseph C. Wyman, July 12, 1982; "Southeast US: Steel Plant Nursery," *Institute for Iron and Steel Studies,* April 1981.

32. George McManus, "Steel Industry Breaking Ranks," *Iron Age,* June 15, 1982.

33. John Savage, "Incentive Programs at Nucor Corporation Boost Productivity," *Personnel Administrator,* August 1981.

34. "Minimill Special Section," *American Metal Market,* December 17, 1982; Thomas F. Boyle, "Forging Ahead: Steel Companies Consider Basic Structural Changes," *Wall Street Journal,* May 27, 1983.

35. "Technology and Steel Industry Competitiveness," Office of Technology Assessment.

36. *Ibid.;* "Analysis of Michigan as the Site for a Small Electric Furnace Mill to Recycle Scrap Into Steel," Industrial Development Division, Institute of Science and Technology, University of Michigan, 1974.

37. Lawrence Stevens, "Designs of the Times," *Inc.,* January 1983.

38. "Industry Census of the Contract Tooling and Machining Industry 1979–80," National Tooling and Machining Association, Washington, DC, January 1981.

5. BANKING ON PEOPLE

1. Phillip I. Blumberg, *The Megacorporation in American Society* (Englewood Cliffs, New Jersey: Prentice-Hall, 1975), pp. 15, 67–70; data from National Federation of Independent Business, research, Washington, DC.

2. Blumberg, *Megacorporation,* pp. 96–97; David Birch and Susan McCracken, *Corporate Evolution,* MIT Program on Neighborhood and Regional Change, January 1981.

3. "A Merger Specialist Who Hates Mergers," *Fortune,* October 19, 1981.

4. W. T. Grimm & Co. reports, Chicago: 1979–82; also cited in *Business Week,* March 29, 1983; Jeffrey Madrick, "Cutting Loose: The Drive to Divest," *New York Times,* July 3, 1983.

5. Mary Greenbaum, "Making the Most of Unnoticed Assets," *Fortune,* June 15, 1981; "Why Leveraged Buyouts Are Getting So Hot," *Business Week,* June 27, 1983.

6. *Business Week,* June 27, 1983.

7. "Life Begins at Sixty," *Fortune,* November 10, 1980.

8. Louis M. Hacker, *The Course of American Economic Growth and Development* (New York: John Wiley, 1970), p. 130.

9. Stuart W. Bruchey, ed., *Small Business in American Life* (New York: Columbia University Press, 1980), p. 244; Paul B. Trescott, *Financing American Enterprise* (New York: Harper & Row, 1963), pp. 36–37.

10. *Ibid.,* p. 97; Blumberg, *Megacorporation in American Society,* p. 226.

11. James Vitarello, "Public Pension Fund/Local Bank Partnerships Provide Financing for Small Business Development" (draft paper for *Governmental Finance,* September 1983).

12. *Ibid.;* Tracy Herrick, "Small Banks a Growth Industry," published privately.

13. "1981 Results for 405 Chicago Area Banks," *Crain's Chicago Business,* June 21, 1982.

14. Bob Graham, "Economic Goal: To Diversify," "Miami: Capital

of Latin America," *Advertising Age,* November 30, 1981; see also *New York Times,* May 23, 1982.

15. *Texas Fact Book 1980,* Bureau of Business Research, University of Texas, Austin, 1980; Herrick, *op. cit.;* Morgenson and Green, consultant report, 1983.

16. Mark Gladstone, "Quick Profits Spark Boom in New Banks," *Los Angeles Times,* February 16, 1983.

17. Martin Barron, "Fewer But Bigger Banks Seen by 1990," *Los Angeles Times,* June 22, 1983.

18. Patrick Boyle, "Prosperity Seen for Small Banks in Era of Giants," *Los Angeles Times,* April 17, 1983.

19. Reed Hayes, "The Story of the Bank of Italy and A. P. Giannini," *San Francisco Chronicle,* April 30, 1928.

20. *Ibid.*

21. Marquis James and Bessie James, *Biography of a Bank* (New York: Harper & Row, 1954).

22. Reed Hayes, *San Francisco Chronicle,* April 30, 1928.

23. *Ibid.*

24. *Ibid.*

25. Julian Dana, *A. P. Giannini: Giant of the West* (New York: Prentice-Hall, 1947), pp. 358–74.

26. Victor Zunana and Kathryn Christensen, "At Bank America, A New Regime Strives to Reverse Declines," *Wall Street Journal,* May 20, 1982.

27. "Armacost Jolts B of A Out of Its Complacency," *Los Angeles Times,* June 6, 1982.

28. *Ibid.*

29. *State of Small Business,* Small Business Administration, Government Printing Office, Washington, DC: 1983.

30. Figures cited in *Venture Economics,* 1980.

31. Figures cited in *Venture Capital Journal,* May 1980.

32. Figures cited in *Pensions and Investment Age,* January 19, 1981; *Venture Capital Journal.*

33. Andrew Feinberg, "Fifty Who Made Millions," *Venture,* April 1983.

34. "The Venture Capital 100," *Venture,* June 1983.
35. Gene Bylinsky, *The Innovation Millionaires* (New York: Scribners, 1976), pp. 3–11.
36. Thomas P. Murphy, "The Art of Raising Children," *Forbes,* May 15, 1977; Textron Financial Statements, 1975–80.
37. Frank R. Kline, "Venture Capital High Technology Prospects for the Future," Pacific Technology Venture Fund, paper presented October 20, 1982, Hotel Okura, Tokyo, Japan.
38. Feinberg, "Fifty Who Made Millions"; "The Venture 100: Getting Ready for the Good Times," *Venture,* May 1983.

6. AMERICA AS NUMBER ONE

1. "Will U.S. Shut the Door on Immigrants?" *U.S. News and World Report,* April 12, 1981.
2. Estimates provided by Consul-General of Japan, Los Angeles.
3. Eui-Young Yu, Earl H. Phillips, and Eun Sik Yang, *Koreans in Los Angeles: Prospects and Promises* (Los Angeles: Koyro Research Institute, 1982), p. 80.
4. John Franklin Sugg, "Miami: 'Capital of Latin America'," *Advertising Age,* November 30, 1981.
5. Barry Siegel, "Immigrants: Sizing up the New Wave," *Los Angeles Times,* December 12, 1982.
6. Arnold C. Cooper and William Dunkelberg, "A New Look at Business Entry: Experiences of 1805 Entrepreneurs" (draft paper); Robert Pear, "Immigration Study Surprises," *Los Angeles Herald-Examiner,* September 22, 1980.
7. "Some Who Made It in a New Land," *U.S. News and World Report,* April 12, 1982.
8. "What the World Thinks of America," *Newsweek,* July 11, 1983.
9. "The International Microelectronic Challenge," *Semiconductor Industry Association,* May 1981, pp. 5, 11; Michael Borrus with James Millstein and John Zysman, "Responses to the Japanese Challenge in High Technology: Innovation, Maturity, and U.S.–Japanese Competition in Micro-electronics,"

Berkeley Roundtable on the International Economy, University of California, Berkeley, 1983.

10. Japan External Trade Organization (JETRO), "Japanese Manufacturing Operations in the United States," JETRO, New York, September 1981.

11. "Lure of the Golden West," *German International*, August 8, 1979; Michael Borrus, James Millstein and John Zysman, *U.S.-Japanese Competition in the Semiconductor Industry*, Institute of International Studies, University of California, Berkeley, 1981.

12. JETRO, "Japanese Manufacturing Operations in the United States"; and biotechnology firms compiled by Yoriko Kishimoto, editor, *Biotechnology in Japan Newsletter*, Palo Alto, California.

13. President's Commission for a National Agenda for the Eighties, *The Quality of American Life in the Eighties* (Washington, DC: 1980), p. 41; Doyle McManus, "Future's Not What It Used to Be in U.S.," *Los Angeles Times*, December 30, 1982.

14. *Ibid.;* President's Commission, *The Quality of American Life in the Eighties*, p. 103.

15. Ira C. Magaziner and Robert B. Reich, *Minding America's Business* (New York: Law and Business, 1981), pp. 13–14.

16. Yankelovich, Skelly, and White, "Meeting the Japanese Challenge: The Need for Leadership," report prepared for Motorola, 1982, pp. 6–13.

17. Bennett Harrison and Barry Blueston, *The Deindustrialization of America* (New York: Basic Books, 1982), p. 13.

18. Ezra F. Vogel, *Japan as Number One* (New York: Harper & Row, 1980), p. 254.

19. *Ibid.,* p. 113–17.

20. Magaziner and Reich, *Minding America's Business,* pp. 6, 65.

21. Robert B. Reich, *America's Next Frontier* (New York: Times Books, 1983), p. 279.

22. Editorial on Industrial Policy, *Reason,* August 1983.

23. "Future's Not What It Used to Be in U.S.," *Los Angeles Times,* December 30, 1982.

24. Martin Weiner, *English Culture and the Decline of the Industrial Spirit: 1850–1980* (Cambridge, UK: Cambridge University Press, 1981), p. 160.

25. Andrew Hacker, *The End of the American Era* (New York: Atheneum, 1971), pp. 227–28.

26. Joseph Schumpeter, *Capitalism, Socialism and Democracy* (New York: Harper & Row, 1947), p. 124.

27. Carlo M. Cipolla, *Before the Industrial Revolution,* 2nd edition (New York: Norton, 1980), pp. 158–92; Fernand Braudel, *Capitalism and Material Life, 1400–1800* (New York: Harper & Row, 1973), pp. 263, 277, 283, 302–3.

28. Thomas S. Ashton, *The Industrial Revolution* (London: Oxford University Press, 1961), p. 9.

29. *Ibid.,* p. 14.

30. Eric J. Hobsbawm, *The Age of Revolution: 1789–1848* (New York: New American Library, 1962), pp. 165–73.

31. Weiner, *English Culture and the Decline of the Industrial Spirit: 1850–1980,* p. 14; Louis M. Hacker, *The Course of American Economic Growth and Development,* p. 135; Robert K. Webb, *Modern England* (New York: Dodd, Mead, 1968), p. 378; Jonathan Hughes, *Industrialization and Economic History* (New York: McGraw-Hill, 1970), pp. 130–37.

32. Rosalind Williams, "Reindustrialization Past and Present," *Technology Review,* November 12, 1982.

33. Charles F. Sabel, *Work and Politics* (Cambridge, UK: Cambridge University Press, 1982), p. 29.

34. John Tipple, *The Crisis of the American Dream* (New York: Pegasus, 1968), p. 199.

35. Webb, *Modern England,* pp. 567–68; Douglas F. LaMont, *Foreign State Enterprises* (New York: Basic Books, 1979), pp. 54–57.

36. Gustav Stolper, Karl Hauser and Knut Borchardt, translated by Toni Stolper, *The German Economy: 1870 to the Present* (New

York: Harcourt, Brace & World, 1967), pp. 260–61, 223; John Zysman, *Finance and the Politics of Industrial Change* (draft paper), University of California, Berkeley, pp. 334–37.

37. "U.S. Direct Investment Abroad in 1980," *Survey of Current Business,* August 1981.

38. Zysman, *Finance and the Politics of Industrial Change,* pp. 204–5.

39. "Can Mitterrand Remake France's Economy?" *Business Week,* January 10, 1983; Michael Landers, "France, Inc.," *Industry Week,* April 5, 1982.

40. Magaziner and Reich, *Minding America's Business,* pp. 279–81.

41. "Technology Gives the U.S. a Big Edge," *Business Week,* August 23, 1982; "AEG's Failure Spells Trouble," *Business Week,* June 30, 1980.

42. "Europe lags behind in world race to develop biotechnology," *European Chemical News,* October 18, 1982; Commission of the European Communities, "The Competitiveness of the Community Industry," (Luxembourg: 1982), pp. 33, 94.

43. *Ibid.,* pp. 24–25, 94; Robert J. Samuelson, "Europe's Economy Is Really the Pits," *Los Angeles Times,* March 28, 1983; "Chilling Climate for U.S. Investment," *Business Week,* December 7, 1981.

44. Stephen Kindel and Rosemary Brady, "Creative Chaos," *Forbes,* December 20, 1983.

45. "Italy's Hidden Strengths," *World Press Review,* April 1983; Stephen Kindel and Rosemary Brady, "The Wave of the Future?" *Forbes,* December 20, 1983.

46. "Italy's Hidden Strengths," *op. cit.*

47. James Buxton, "Danielli gets maximum from mini-mills," *Financial Times,* November 2, 1982; John Tagliabue, "Her Job: Building Steel Mills," *New York Times,* January 12, 1982.

48. *Financial Times,* April 17, 1982; Commission of the European Communities, *op. cit.,* p. 92.

49. Michael G. Landers, "France, Inc.," *Industry Week,* April 5, 1982; Lawrence Minard, "A Chat with Fernand Braudel," *Forbes,* June 11, 1982.

50. Lawrence Minard, "A Touch of Capitalism," *Forbes,* May 9, 1983; "Recession spurs an entrepreneurial spirit," *Business Week,* September 21, 1981.

51. Sol Sanders, *Honda: The Man and His Machines* (Boston: Little, Brown, 1975), pp. 55, 62.

52. G. C. Allen, *A Short Economic History of Modern Japan* (New York: St. Martin's Press, 1981), p. 234.

53. Ashton, *The Industrial Revolution,* p. 11.

54. Hiroshi Kato, "The Japanese Venture Business," *Securities Analyst Journal,* March 1982.

55. Sanders, *op. cit.,* xv.

56. John G. Roberts, *The Mitsui Empire: Three Centuries of Japanese Business* (New York: Weatherhill, 1973), pp. 12, 20–36.

57. Paul Wilkin, *Entrepreneurship* (Norwood, New Jersey: Ablex, 1979), p. 184.

58. Allen, *op. cit.,* p. 114.

59. Roberts, *op. cit.,* pp. 264, 306; Kazuo Kawai, *Japan's American Interlude* (Chicago: University of Chicago Press, 1974), pp. 154–55.

60. Kawai, *op. cit.*

61. Roberts, *op. cit.,* p. 417; Allen, *op. cit.,* p. 238.

62. "Expertise for Sale," *Forbes,* October 25, 1982.

63. Terutomo Ozawa, *Japan's Technological Challenge to the West, 1950-1974: Motivation and Accomplishment* (Cambridge, Mass.: MIT Press, 1974), p. 2.

64. William Rapp, "The United States and Japan: Competition in World Markets," speech presented at Washington Hilton Hotel, March 21, 1980 (copyright: The Association for Asian Studies, 1980).

65. Ira C. Magaziner and Thomas M. Hout, "Japanese Industrial Policy," Institute of International Studies, University of California, Berkeley, 1980; Japan Pacific Associates, "Japanese Responses to Export Restrictions" (draft paper), Palo Alto, California, March 16, 1983; Allen, *A Short Economic History of Modern Japan,* p. 267.

66. Nick Lyons, *The Sony Vision* (New York: Crown Publishers, 1976), pp. 42–43; "Industrial Policy in Japan" (New York: Japan Trade Center, 1983).

67. Frank Gibney, *Japan: The Fragile Superpower* (New York: New American Library, 1979), p. 355; Sanders, *Honda: The Man and His Machines,* p. 173.

68. Ministry of International Trade and Industry, "The Vision of MITI Policies in the 1980s," Tokyo, March 17, 1980, p. 7.

69. "Japan's New Crop of Young Pragmatists," *Focus Japan,* November 1982.

70. Japan Pacific Associates, "Japanese Responses to Export Restrictions"; Thomas Rohlen, "The Pacific Basin: Economic Interdependence and Issues for the Future," Background Paper for the Mansfield Center for Pacific Affairs, 1982.

71. Takashi Nakjima, President, Sumitomo Metal America, Letter to the Editor, *American Metal Market,* July 7, 1982; Sam Jameson, "MITI Policy Irks Japanese Investors," *Los Angeles Times,* March 21, 1983; Edward Boyer, "How Japan Manages Declining Industries," *Fortune,* July 10, 1983.

72. "Japan Inc. Goes International with High Technology," *Business Week,* December 14, 1981.

73. Frank R. Kline, "Venture Capital: High Technology Prospects for the Future," Pacific Technology Venture Fund, paper presented October 20, 1982, Hotel Okura, Tokyo; Uchihatsi Katsuto, "The Research Gap," *World Press Review,* April 1983.

74. Katsuto, *op. cit.;* "The information era beckons," *World Business Weekly,* September 14, 1981.

75. Ministry of International Trade and Industry, "White Paper on Small and Medium Enterprises in Japan, 1982" (Tokyo: MITI, 1982), p. 103.

76. John Marcom, Jr., "Japan Turning to U.S. Models," *The Asian Wall Street Journal,* May 31, 1982.

7. TWENTY-FIRST CENTURY CAPITALISM

1. Robert R. Palmer, *The Age of Democratic Revolution,* Volume One (Princeton, New Jersey: Princeton University Press, 1969), p. 253.
2. Jean-Jacques Servan-Schreiber, "Computers: A World Renaissance Is Within Reach," *Los Angeles Times,* Opinion Section, July 12, 1981.
3. Thomas Pursell, ed., *Readings in Technology and American Life* (New York: Oxford University Press, 1969), p. 353.
4. Joseph Schumpeter, *Capitalism, Socialism and Democracy* (New York: Harper & Row, 1947), xi.
5. John Naisbitt, speech to Association for Humanistic Psychology, Los Angeles Conference, September 1, 1981.
6. Statistics compiled by Yoriko Kishimoto, Japan Pacific Associates.
7. Martin Weiner, *English Culture and the Decline of the Industrial Spirit: 1850-1980* (Cambridge, UK: Cambridge University Press, 1981), p. 130.
8. *Ibid.,* p. 157.
9. Colin Norman, "Microelectronics at Work: Production and Jobs in the World Economy," *Worldwatch* Paper #39, October 1980, p. 40.
10. John Zysman, "Policy for a Period of Industrial Challenge," Berkeley Roundtable on the International Economy (BRIE), University of California, 1983 (unpublished paper), p. 18.
11. Michael Borrus, James Millstein, and John Zysman, *U.S.-Japanese Competition in the Semiconductor Industry,* Institute of International Studies, University of California (Berkeley, 1981), p. 13.
12. *Ibid.,* p. 38.
13. *Ibid.,* p. 5.
14. Tom Redburn, "U.S., Japan Wage Battle of Chips," *Los Angeles Times,* May 24, 1983.
15. Donald K. White, "Japan on Offense—Bland Smile Disappearing," *San Francisco Chronicle,* April 8, 1980.

16. Louis Kehoe, "The Chips are Down in California," *Financial Times,* February 5, 1982.
17. Michael Borrus, "Responses to the Japanese Challenge in High Technology," Tables 6 and 10a (draft paper).
18. *Ibid.,* Table 2.
19. *Ibid.,* p. 6.
20. Redburn, *op. cit.*
21. John Zysman, "Japanese Technology Development" (draft paper), Berkeley.
22. "America Cannot Afford Its Cost of Capital," *The Economist,* April 30, 1983.
23. George Hatsopoulous, "High Cost of Capital: Handicap of American Industry," paper prepared for American Business Conference, April 26, 1983.
24. *Ibid.*
25. Bennett Harrison and Barry Blueston, *The Deindustrialization of America* (New York: Basic Books, 1982), p. 198.
26. Lawrence Litvak, *Pension Funds and Economic Renewal* (Council of State Planning Agencies, Washington, 1982), pp. 1–2.
27. *Ibid.,* p. 9.
28. "The New Entrepreneurs," *Business Week,* April 18, 1983.
29. Borrus, *op. cit.,* pp. 100–3.
30. *Ibid.,* p. 98.
31. "The IRS Takes a Hard Line on Software," *Business Week,* May 2, 1983; M. S. Forbes, "Shortsighted Ruling," *Forbes,* May 9, 1983.
32. Assistance provided here by Ken Haggerty, American Electronics Association, from upcoming study.
33. Kathy Kristof, "Crusading CPA Coaxes Congress to Adopt Investor Tax-Deferral Plan," *Los Angeles Times,* June 19, 1983; Mo Mehlsak, "Small Business Bill Languishes in Committee," *Daily News,* July 29, 1983.
34. Candace E. Trunzo, "The New Millionaires," *Money,* January 1981.
35. John Hubner, "Ask Not What Computers Can Do For Your

Country," *San Jose Mercury Sunday Magazine,* February 27, 1983.

36. Security Pacific National Bank, The Futures Research Unit, "Capitalism Goes Into Orbit" (no date).

37. Figures based on 1975 study, Chase Econometrics Associates; Thomas G. Donlan, "The High Frontier," *Barrons,* June 8, 1981.

38. George C. Lodge and William R. Glass, "Making American Strategy in a Competitive World," Graduate School of Business Administration, Division of Research, Harvard University, October 24, 1982, p. 3.

39. Hubner, *op. cit.; Venture,* April 1983.

40. Karl Marx and Friedrich Engels, "The Communist Manifesto," from *The Essential Left* (New York: Barnes & Noble, 1961), p. 20.

41. Schumpeter, *Capitalism, Socialism and Democracy,* p. 134.

42. Theodore K. Quinn, *Giant Business: Threat to Democracy* (New York: Exposition Press, 1954), p. 130.

43. Paul Jacobs and Saul Landau, eds., *The New Radicals* (New York: Vintage, 1966), p. 154.

44. Daniel Yankelovich, *New Rules* (New York: Random House, 1981), p. 232.

45. "Work: Changing Motivations and Values," *Trends,* Futures Research Unit, Security Pacific National Bank, October 1978.

46. Tove Helland Hammer and Robert N. Stern, "Employee Ownership: Implications for the Organizational Distribution of Power," *Academy of Management Journal,* Volume 23, Number 1, p. 79.

47. Thomas B. Rosenstiel, "Why Do Firms Make More When Workers Own Stock?" *Peninsula Times Tribune,* October 22, 1982.

48. Robert M. Kaus, "The Trouble With Unions," *Harper's,* June 1983.

49. Rosenstiel, *op. cit.*

50. List of companies compiled by Steve Coll, Community Infor-

mation Project, and Corey Rosen and Katherine Klein, National Center for Employee Ownership.

51. Allan Sloan, "Go Forth and Compete!" *Forbes,* November 23, 1981.

52. Irwin Ross, "What Happens When Employees Buy a Company," *Fortune,* June 2, 1980.

53. Allen Beckenstein, Robert Coffey and Mark Weaver, "University Resources for Small Business Research," paper prepared for National Federation of Independent Business, Washington, DC, 1978.

54. Bennett Harrison and Barry Blueston, *The Deindustrialization of America,* p. 150.

55. Cato Policy Report, January 1981; "How the Classroom Turns Out Entrepreneurs," *Business Week,* June 18, 1979.

56. Richard King, "The MBA in Small Business: Wise Investment or Big Mistake?" (draft paper for *Harvard Business Review*), January 24, 1983.

57. "The Colossus That Works," *Time,* July 11, 1983.

58. Kathleen K. Weigner, "Signs of Life," *Forbes,* June 7, 1982.

59. G. E. Hardymon, M. J. DeNino, M. S. Salter, "When Corporate Venture Capital Doesn't Work," *Harvard Business Review,* May–June 1983.

60. "The New Entrepreneurs," *Business Week,* April 18, 1983.

61. "What's Wrong at Exxon Enterprises," *Business Week,* August 24, 1981.